The Demise of the Liberal Tradition

Two essays on the future of British university adult education

Alastair D. Crombie

Gwyn Harries-Jenkins

LEEDS STUDIES
IN ADULT AND CONTINUING EDUCATION

First published in 1983 in the series
Leeds Studies in Adult and Continuing Education
by the University of Leeds, Department of
Adult and Continuing Education
Leeds LS2 9JT

Leeds Studies in Adult and Continuing Education
ISSN 0261–1406

The Demise of the Liberal Tradition
ISBN 0 907644 02 3

Set in 10 on 12 point Times Roman
and printed in Great Britain by J. Jackman and Co.
Chancellor Street, Leeds LS6 2TG

Contents

University adult education into the 1980s

Gwyn Harries-Jenkins

Introduction

In contemporary discussions about the role and function of university extramural departments, one of the more important questions which arises is whether there is anything provided by the traditional university department which could not be provided more effectively, more efficiently, and more cheaply by an alternative agency. It is not a simple question for it involves not only issues of resource allocation and the rational ordering of curricula, but also debates about values and historical tradition. The latter in particular die hard but any enquiry has to go beyond statements about the glories of the past to look more critically at two themes which are implicit in the question.

First, the debate is about the possibility of the alternative provision of adult education courses by some other *external* agency, that is, we have to question whether other structured educational institutions in the public sector such as polytechnics, colleges of higher or further education, adult education institutes and so on, or other bodies such as the Open University or the Workers' Educational Association are better able to meet present-day needs of adult students.

Secondly, we are led to ask whether within the traditional university structure, the retention of a separate department of extramural studies can be justified, or whether the responsibility for course provision should be transferred to either an internal department or some part of the administrative machinery. In other words, the question is whether an *internal* agency can effectively accept responsibility in this field.

The importance of these basic questions should not be overlooked. Although we are essentially concerned with the university sector, the possibility of transferring responsibility for course provision in this sector of education has considerable implications for all agencies which are

1

currently working in the field. If the rationale of tried and proven university provision can be questioned, then there is no reason to suppose that the untried and often speculative provision proposed by other agencies will be exempt from evaluation. At the same time, debate about the future role of university extramural departments is now particularly apposite. In a period when considerable economic constraints are imposed upon universities as a whole — to the extent that some internal departments are at risk — the identification of what ought to be done by extramural departments to justify their use of scarce resources is a significant question. The need to justify the retention of these departments within academic institutions which are forced to look critically at priorities within their areas of teaching, research and administration thus encourages a careful examination of the potential aims and objectives of university adult education.

The traditional role

The conventional explanation for the retention (if not indeed the development) of the extramural department, is very much dependent on the maintenance of the liberal tradition. Traditionally, one of the defining characteristics of British adult education has been its identification with a liberal-progressive movement. In the formative years of development, the existence of this movement was very much prized. It was seen as a challenge which spurred on both tutors and taught to greater efforts, the effects of which, as the 'Carnegie Report' of 1928 implied, were thought to have beneficial results:

> But it can scarcely be denied that there is a real movement for adult education in existence today — inchoate, perhaps, but nevertheless, extensive, and offering a challenge of fundamental importance to those responsible for the educational provision of the country. This challenge must be met. The effect of adult education in the opening up of new interests for the students, in cultivating their powers of appreciation and enjoyment, in developing critical judgement, in training for creative leadership — all this is so important to the community that it is necessary to consider the problem afresh and to treat it on broader lines than has hitherto been the case.[1]

This perception of adult education as a form of liberal, non-vocational education, rather than as the *education of adults* was a consistent feature of discussion and debate in this sector of education. It was a characteristic which was seemingly as descriptive of the aims of university provision as of those of local authority provision. Even so, this interpretation of the purposes of adult education was heavily biased towards the work of the so-called 'Responsible Bodies', and, in the traditional sense, the importance of other institutions as providers of adult education did tend to be overlooked.

It was, in essence, a progressive movement which believed that in the contemporary educational setting university adult education in general, and the tutorial class in particular, would encourage the work of a thoughtful and dedicated minority of students who were destined to become civic leaders. As A. L. Smith put it in his introduction to the '1919 Report':

> the millions of rank and file can certainly get the two educational essentials which will enable them to recognise those natural leaders; these two essentials being (a) the development of an open habit of mind, clear-sighted and truth-loving, proof against sophisms, shibboleths, clap trap phrases and cant; (b) the possession of certain elementary information and essential facts about such main questions as the Empire, the relations between Capital and Labour, the relations between science and production, and other such subjects.[2]

What Kelly, in comparing the 1919 Report and the Russell Report, terms the naive 'idealism' of the former sums up clearly the ethos of adult education in the formative years of this liberal-progressive movement.[3] It was an ethos, the central core beliefs of which reflected the assumption that in seeking to effect social change, liberal rationalism, whose achievements had already been so marked, led the way. As Rex Warner points out, the seemingly unquestionable validity of this assumption led to a situation in which

> among the intelligentsia it was accepted as an axiom that all that was necessary to ensure a continuous growth of happiness and prosperity for all the world was to be reasonable and reasonably moral, a task well within the powers of everyone.[4]

The perception of rationality, however, was in reality a value-orien-

3

tated assessment which equated the objectives of liberal adult education with the desire to create a just and open society. This would seemingly be effected by reforming unacceptable facets of the existing social system. It was, therefore, an ethos which sought repeatedly to facilitate the participation of hitherto excluded individuals in the exercise of power within that system. Consequently, this aim did not equate with the objectives of social revolution, that is, with the overthrow or dissolution of the existing system and its replacement by an alternative mode of social organisation. Equally the liberal-progressive movement rejected the identification of adult education with utilitarianism and with courses designed for technical and vocational purposes.[5] Kelly makes the point very clearly:

> At a time when many adult education movements were tending to drift in the direction of technical and vocational education, when even the working men's colleges were finding it difficult to resist the general trend, the universities clearly restated the concept of liberal study. In doing so they did not neglect the vocational needs of the students but they insisted that even studies directed to vocational ends should be undertaken in a broad humane spirit, and that the fundamental values and purposes of human life should be kept steadily in view. Thereby the universities established a tradition of liberal study which has ever since been the distinctive mark and special pride of English adult education.[6]

The dominance of the progressive, liberal movement within adult education has hitherto been most marked. It has reflected in part a concern for excellence which recognised the worth of a certain educational ethos — the Oxbridge idea of the cultivated, literary, gentleman scholar who pursued his studies through close contact with the best academic minds, through lively exchanges of class discussion, and through independent written work.[7] This concern for excellence invited acrimonious debate and discussion about the maintenance of standards. It encouraged the development of a model of adult education which was largely based on a conception of education as something which was gentlemanly, non-utilitarian and largely ornamental. The extreme goals of this model were admirably summed up by T. S. Eliot when he wrote that 'The first task of the community should be the preservation of education within the cloisters uncontaminated by the deluge of barbarism outside'.[8] Eliot, however, was not alone in his interpretation of the goals of education, and a common theme among adult educationists who were supporters of the liberal model was their dislike of a contemporary 'mechanised, commercialised, industrialised existence'.[9]

Some of the arguments which can be used to justify the existence of this model have been admirably analysed by Flann Campbell, although it would be incorrect to interpret his comments on 'Latin and the Elite Tradition in Education' to mean that liberal adult education is primarily or solely concerned with the teaching of classics or classical studies.[10] What his analysis of the élite tradition in education shows, however, is the manner in which this tradition is derived from a philosophy which identifies education with preparation for leadership.

Here we discover a clear relationship between the classical interpretation of the aims of general education and the stylised model of traditional adult education which made civic responsibility one of the central purposes of course provision. In one sense the concept of a 'humane' education is that of personal development, and the case was neatly epitomised in the reference by the 'Interim Report' (1918) of the Adult Education Committee to individual motivation:

> The motive which impels men and women to seek education is partly the wish for fuller personal development. It arises from the desire for knowledge, for self-expression, for the satisfaction of intellectual, aesthetic and spiritual needs, and for a fuller life. It is based upon a claim for the recognition of human personality.[11]

Nevertheless we cannot overlook the fact that the Adult Education Committee wished to extend this restricted identification of liberal adult study with 'humane' education. It did so by transmuting the ideal of leadership into that of civic responsibility and by arguing that the latter was an essential purpose of the education of free citizens. The link between personal development and social purpose established itself as a relatively uncontroversial item of the liberal adult education tradition.

The extended definition of the aims and objectives of 'liberal' adult education, moreover, not only stressed the importance of an appreciation of the responsibilities of citizenship, of the significance of political, social and industrial ideals and of a growing determination to realise them. It also institutionalised the teaching methodology. Consequently, a situation was all too frequently met in which it was argued that the preferred subjects of liberal adult education were to be taught in a preferred way. This often produced a somewhat paradoxical situation in which an insistence on the freedom of the tutor and student to determine the interest or relevance of the selected subject was balanced by dogmatic assertions as to the 'right' way to teach those subjects.

One practical effect of this is noted by Jackson. He suggests that very many adult educators, in considering critically the dimensions of the liberal progressive movement,

> remember scores of self-congratulatory conferences in which the virtues of liberal adult education were extolled; its freedom and open debate; its rigour combined with relaxed presentation; the friendly relationship between teachers and students who joined together in a disinterested search after truth.[12]

In many respects, this self-indulgence was a confirmation of a myth and although the aims and objectives of the liberal-progressive movement may have been readily accepted in the past, we are now entering a period when we sense that the movement is increasingly subject to critical analysis. Yet, as a matter of fact, this assessment is no new phenomenon. Questions were being asked about the validity of the movement some fifty years ago:

> What went wrong, then? Alas, liberalism stuck at the last fence and, as it were, handed on its torch to socialism over the top of a barrier, which, for liberalism, was insuperable. The great society of mankind, free and equal, the dream of philosophers and scholars, was at last becoming a practical possibility, and up to this point liberal rational-ism had led the way. Now arose the question of bringing into existence the social organisation appropriate to the great ideal. This organisation was a classless society, and liberalism shrank back aghast. It had come to the end of its tether, and has remained there. Let us say nothing but good about the dead. Liberal rationalism had a long and splendid life. But it is important to remember that its legitimate offspring and successor, the heir indeed to all the ages, is socialism.[13]

This kind of criticism, however, was essentially political in shape. Now we have more general evidence of a swing away from what can be seen as a former over-readiness to accept without question the validity of the liberal thesis. Given that the thesis was accepted in the past without discussion, we have to consider in the 1980s those declarations of intent which imply that, notwithstanding the rich cultural and historical traditions of adult education, a newly-evolved set of objectives can be established which more properly reflect the needs of contemporary society.

The decline of the liberal tradition

In contemporary society there would appear to be growing evidence of the general decline of the liberal-progressive ideology. The innovations and alterations of our everyday life since the turn of the century have been very considerable. To list the forms or to stress the extent of such change would be to emphasise the commonplace. Over time, an element of change seem inevitable, yet what is now happening to the boundaries and characteristics of the traditional liberal-progressive ideology goes beyond that which has been hitherto experienced. This change is something more than mere innovation or improvement, for the apparent demise of the liberal tradition is seemingly an attack on the very foundation of a deeply cherished political and moral ideology.

One sign of this shift is the manner in which it is now accepted with but few reservations that the relationship of the state to society has altered immeasurably. In the sphere of our economic life we witness the increasing involvement of government in the affairs of the nation. A very large part of all economic activity is now controlled by the state, and that is not regarded even by conservatives as socialism. Equally, political life in the United Kingdom appears to be encountering growing demands for the adoption of more positive — if not more extreme — ideological stances. Such demands impose a considerable strain on those attributes such as tolerance, balance and equality of treatment, which have always been identified as defining characteristics of the liberal-progressive ideology.

Although neutrality in politics is a contradiction in terms, the strength of the traditional belief system has lain hitherto in its identification with a framework for debate which implies a willingness to accept consensus. It has assumed a cohesion and stability in politics which emphasise not the struggle for power and privilege, but the significance of norms and behavioural standards in the regulation of political life. Modern pressures, in contrast, can be judged to emphasise the interests of various individuals and groups within society. The needs and desires of these factions, rather than concern for the wellbeing of society as a whole, seemingly motivate attitudes towards the division of power and privilege. One conclusion is that the liberal-progressive ideology no longer offers a plausible response to contemporary social discontents.

What I am concerned with in this essay, however, is something more specific than an assessment of trends in the parent society — notwithstanding the importance of socio-ecological variables as determinants of planning in the field of education. What this essay sets out to analyse is the direction and degree of change in the policy and practice of university adult education. It begins from the premise that although the liberal-progressive movement succeeded in the past in making sense of society in educational terms it is now subject to an increasing amount of criticism. These pressures are related not only to the questioning of the liberal experience which draws heavily on *ideological* awareness, they relate also, at a more pragmatic level, to contemporary assumptions about the *management* of formal educational systems.

To facilitate this broader educational analysis, I propose that the liberal-progressive school of higher adult education can be (and in fact is being) challenged on three basic counts:

(i) the traditional means of implementing such a programme can no longer be accepted unquestioningly;

(ii) the demand for improved management rationality in adult education materially affects the continued provision of liberal studies;

(iii) the traditional liberal claim to provide for the real 'needs' and 'wants' of adult learners is no longer realistic and invites criticism on a number of fronts.

These objections emphasise the importance of distinguishing between the ethos of the liberal-progressive movement and a more precise concern with aims and objectives resulting from the existence of the university system itself.

The liberal movement, it can be argued, is too often representative of a pernicious form of obscurantism. It starts from a self-usage of 'university adult education' which equates objectives with the dreams of

Jude the Obscure. What this means in the context of contemporary assessment is that one is made very aware of the impact upon adult education of discussion and policy documents written in terms that more or less ensure that all responses will respect the framework of an educational philosophy enunciated many years ago. This also suggests that we need to escape from a purely historical approach to the growth and development of liberal adult education. This change of direction accepts that a persistent feature of British adult education in the past has been the almost total autonomy enjoyed by programme planners, tutors and students in decisions about core syllabuses and curricula. Free from the shackles of examination demands, they have sought to frame a set of proposals which would ensure the maximum liberty to students. The aim, indeed, seemed to be one which ensured that although the state should aid education, it should leave wide powers of self-organisation to those whom it aids. A covenant has been preserved over many years: 'This tradition, though it does not make for administrative symmetry, we believe to be sound'.[14] One effect of this is that adult education in Great Britain is provided by a large number of formal and informal organisations; and because there has never been a comprehensive service for adult education, it is tempting to conclude that 'the involved organisational pattern is only understandable if viewed in terms of the historical development of its parts'.[15]

I do not wish to argue the merits or otherwise of an historical approach, but I would suggest that there is a very real danger in adopting such an approach to the objectives of adult education of overlooking the significance of other factors. A purely historical approach, for example, often ignores the extent to which the objectives of adult education are determined *not* by some reference to impersonal criteria but to the subjective wishes of an individual or individuals who control the distribution of scarce resources. These can be identified as baronial figures of power. Alternatively, they can be seen as reflections of the contemporary ethos. In either case, their influence and importance does suggest that a critical analysis of the liberal-progressive movement merits as wide an approach as is compatible with methodological rigour and empirical evidence.

The traditional adult education class

Much of the criticism of the social and educational aims of the traditional liberal adult education movement revolves around a specific appreciation of the role and function of the adult class. The defining characteristics of the latter, not only as a medium of instruction but also as the determinant of a whole pattern of provision, were clearly spelt out in what can be termed 'The Raybould programme':

> The fundamental plans, adopted as a matter of principle, and for general application in the Department's work ... are that the university's contribution to adult education should be one appropriate to a university, and not only one which could equally well be made by other non-university organisations, and that as far as resources permit, extra-mural facilities must be available to all sections of the community .... In practice the implications of this policy for class work have been taken to be that generally speaking the courses provided by the university should be sufficiently sustained — usually three years, and intensive enough to enable work to be done of a standard appropriate for university sponsorship. Shorter courses are not excluded, but except when specifically preparatory to longer ones, are generally provided only for selected students capable of starting their work at a sufficiently high level to attain a satisfactory standard in a relatively short time.[16]

Basically, these are the characteristics of the ideal-type tutorial class, and although John Lowe suggests that 'There is no need to treat the tutorial class as a sacred cow',[17] it is clear that to many tutors and students the university and the WEA tutorial class have a special place in the hierarchy of adult education provision. In addition, the tutorial class *per se* has served as the definitive model for the shorter courses which are referred to above, so that a whole structure of provision has been created with specific and clearly definable characteristics. This structure can be termed the *traditional class*. It continues to dominate the model of liberal adult education in the university and WEA sector. It has been slavishly copied by institutions in the LEA sector. It has crept, almost unnoticed, into the otherwise innovatory schemes of Open

University courses. Indeed, this dominance can also be seen in its adoption for community education work.

There are therefore a number of reasons for the wish on the part of many people in adult education to maintain in being what is to critics of the traditional class an outmoded and ineffective method of educational provision. To some supporters of the system, the historical antecedents of the traditional class give to this work an aura of sanctity which is rarely questioned. To others, their ideological commitment to the provision of such classes reflects a genuine concern with the need to provide liberal adult education for a mass audience rather than an élite. 'The Trade Union Secretary and the "Labour member" need an Oxford education as much, and will use it to as good ends, as the civil servant or the barrister'.[18] To many administrators, the advantages of these classes are that they clearly and readily satisfy the criteria established in the *Further Education Regulations* of 1969 and that they consequently justify the charging of relatively high fees. To others, the attractiveness of the traditional class is that both teaching and participation in it enhance individual status, and thus validate a claim to the recognition by external bodies of the merit of adult education activities.

The complexity of assessing the worth of these classes is considerable. To a large extent, as we have suggested previously, it is a reflection of more general attitudes to the whole question of adult education and social change. Thus to the 'reformer' and the 'conservationist', the liberal adult education class has an important part to play as a means of implementing their educational objectives. The reformer who seeks to ensure that individuals, irrespective of their social class, have the opportunity of participating at all levels in the working of the social system, relies on the traditional class as a most effective means of transmitting the culture and knowledge which is needed by these participants. The conservationist who is preoccupied with the need to preserve the established cultural norms and values of society, equally considers that the traditional class, rather than any other form of educational provision, is the most satisfactory way of promulgating these norms and values. Conversely, it is the 'revolutionary' and the 'maintenance theorist' who are less willing to accept the claims made by the champions of the traditional class. To the former the method and structure of the class inhibits his wish to provide adult education for that section of the population who are not presently reached by conventional class provision.

To the latter, the almost exclusive identification of the traditional class with the subjects of liberal studies means that the class apparently has little relevance to the teaching of less prestigious utilitarian courses.

Myths and realities

If we are to understand this evaluation further and consider more critically the aims and objectives of contemporary liberal adult education, it is necessary to re-examine claims made about the nature of such a class. The ideal-type traditional class is characterised by a number of criteria:

(i) it is confined to the study of liberal subjects;

(ii) it normally extends over one to three sessions, each containing twenty four meetings of two hours duration;

(iii) students enrolled at the commencement of the class are expected to undertake a systematic course of study and to achieve a given number of attendances;

(iv) the high standard of work demanded in the class is evidenced by the written work and reading of the students;

(v) the number of students at starting should not be less than a laid down minimum (formerly eighteen students) nor should it exceed a given maximum (formerly thirty-two);

(vi) there are no examinations, and entry to the class is 'open' to potential students irrespective of their qualifications.

If an established class satisfies these criteria, then by definition it is an inheritor of a long-standing tradition in adult education, the origins of which can be traced back to the evangelism of Rochdale and Longton and to the influence of Mansbridge and Morant or Tawney and Mactavish.

The initial problem which arises, however, is that critics of the claims made by supporters of these classes are sceptical about the extent to which they satisfy, in practice, all these criteria. Published statistics suggest that these classes do not dominate, quantitatively speaking, adult education provision in the manner in which previous arguments would have us believe. Statistics of university provision, for selected years since 1951/52, are given in Table 1.

Table 1
Extramural provision by United Kingdom universities

Session	Long classes	Sessional classes	Terminal and short classes	Residential courses	Total
1951/52	998	1 270	576	—	2 844
1961/62	803	1 836	2 215	653	5 507
1966/67	694	2 141	2 901	796	6 532
1973/74	812	2 785	4 168	1 352	9 117
1979/80	589	3 047	4 471	1 277	9 384
1980/81	375	3 085	4 545	1 378	9 383

Source: *Annual Reports* of Universities Council for Adult Education
Note: 'Long classes': extending over three sessions or more
   'Sessional classes': twenty to twenty-four meetings

The tutorial-type class, for example is shown for 1980/81 to be no more than 4% of the provision outlined in the Table. The *absolute* total of all kinds of provision by university adult education departments for that session was 11,134 courses, of which the longer extramural courses were only 3·4%. Even so, the legacy of the traditional class does linger on in a qualitative sense. Our attention is still drawn to the excellence of classes of comparatively recent times in which the attitudes of students are said to have been comparable to those of the miner-students in the pre-1914 period who could talk of 'having walked in darkness in their isolated colliery villages until the missionaries came from Longton or Burslem to show them the light'.[19]

In this context our attention is drawn to the fundamental weakness of those arguments which have identified 'good' university adult education with the 'tutorial class', from which so much else is said to have derived. The traditional model has always been open to considerable criticism. Five specific arguments can be advanced, each of which is a comment on the listed criteria of the class. First, it is pointed out that although the jewel of the progressive-liberal adult education crown is the class in which students commit themselves to three years of study, the practice has arisen in many universities and WEA districts of allowing additional students to join the longer classes during the second, or more rarely, the third year of their existence. This suggests that a fundamental characteristic of the class, that is, that students should pledge themselves to follow a course of study over an extended period of years, has been seriously breached. If the tutorial-type class is equated in length and ultimate standard of work with the conventional university course (as seemed to be part of the original intention) then clearly it is an unsatisfactory situation if a student is allowed to join part-way through. In what university, it is argued, can a student graduate after having attended only the last year of a three-year degree programme? The practice of adding students to the long class at best debases its claim that it is unique because of its concern with the systematic exposure of its students to a prolonged and structured course of study. At worst, it suggests that the enlarged class is an example of 'culture-drip' in which 'exaggerated and crudified forms of humanistic values, stripped of subtlety, complexity and fertilising paradox'[20] are distributed amongst a group of transient students.

Although this criticism is most readily evidenced by references to the tutorial class as a specific example of the established liberal adult tradition, it is a criticism which can be applied more generally. What it really amounts to is an attack on the concept of student commitment. Too frequently, it is argued, the worth of a course is measured in terms of class numbers and, more particularly, in terms of the rate of attrition. A 'good' class, by definition, is one in which the initial group of students continues to attend week in and week out. Carried to an extreme, we are, it would seem, most impressed by the class which is in its eighth, ninth or tenth year. What this overlooks, however, is what happens to the selected-out students. Is alternative provision made for students who are unable — for a variety of rational reasons — to commit themselves for a lengthy period of attendance? Alternatively, we have to question whether commitment is something more than simply a physical presence within a group of students.

In the second place, therefore, critics of the claims made about the worth of traditional classes look specifically at the issue of standards. In the absence of examinations in these classes, it is contended that the standard achieved by the class cannot be evaluated other than in subjective terms. Most assessment of students takes place on a very informal basis. The means of assessment are equally uncertain. Is the excellence of students to be measured by their written work, verbal expression, books read, participation in group discussion, understanding of the subject, contribution to the maintenance in being of the class, regular attendance or what?

In the evaluation of the class, considerable emphasis has been traditionally placed on the importance of written work. But this, in turn, raises further points. Students are rarely asked to produce work which is looked at by anyone other than their tutor. The latter on the basis of his experience can claim that the standards reached are equivalent to an honours course in the same subject in a university, but this claim is rarely put to the test. It is very doubtful if students would perform satisfactorily in controlled examination conditions. This in itself does not negate the educational achievements of these classes for these can be considerable, but it does suggest that the claim of the traditional class to a special position in a hierarchy of educational achievement is unjustified, or, at best, highly questionable.

A pungent comment on this question of standards was made by Shaw in the Universities Council for Adult Education *Annual Report 1973–74*.[21] Referring back to the campaign of Raybould in the early 1950s to maintain standards in extra-mural work and to Tawney's conclusion in 1948 that some universities 'appeared to be indifferent whether their extra-mural work is of university standard or not', Shaw suggested that standards were declining and that this was evidenced by the tendency to soft-pedal demands for written work or in some cases to make none at all.[22] Shaw's conclusions were not accepted without question, and the ensuing debate about declining standards encouraged considerable discussion about what those standards really were in the past. As early in the development of the traditional class as the spring of 1909, for example, Tawney could complain to Mansbridge that the work of his tutorial classes, except in Rochdale, had been most unsatisfactory.[23] Similarly, it can be questioned how the claim that standards are declining can be reconciled with the growth of examined certificate, diploma, degree and postgraduate courses.

The third general criticism which is made of the claims put forward by supporters of the traditional class is the reaction to those tutors who stress that the fundamental characteristics of such a class, and its advantage over less formal or unstructured activities, is that in the former it is possible to construct a programme of individual student development

15

so that over time 'the improvement in technical detail seems to be miraculous'.[24] The rejoinder to this contention is that there is little, if any, evidence that an improvement in standards of the provision of intellectually satisfying work cannot be achieved in a different kind of educational structure. Moreover, the original decision to lay down regulations governing the length of courses had a convoluted beginning, and was as much administrative as educational. The tutorial class cannot be assumed to have acquired a special reality simply because its length became mandatory. Indeed the requirement for the class member to complete three years of study can be seen as an administrative demand which has been subsequently rationalised, rather than as an educational prerequisite.

Any emphasis on the length of a course as the most significant educational characteristic ignores two factors. Many courses in higher education are now based on a modular structure which does not commit the student to the study of a single subject with one tutor for a specific period of time. The student selects those areas of study of interest to him or her and has the opportunity of coming into contact with other tutors and students. The encounter is with specialist subject teachers rather than with generalists, and at the same time the boundaries of the student group are extended — two developments that could be said to have distinct educational advantages.

In addition, other courses in higher education which are specifically provided for mature students have successfully avoided this over-emphasis on the total length of the course as the prime indicator of student commitment. Thus the Open University has adopted a policy of open entry to studies (in the best adult education tradition), but it has also incorporated considerable flexibility in the timetabling of its courses. So a student, within limits, decides for himself the length of time for which he is committed, and, most important, it is possible for the individual to 'miss' a year of study without incurring any penalty or fatally disrupting the educational experience. Such a policy contrasts very markedly with the explicit claims of conventional 'class' purism that the student must undertake to follow a course of study over a prescribed period of time. Yet it would be very injudicious to conclude that the marked success of the Open University is associated with a form of provision visibly inferior in structural terms to that of the traditional liberal, non-vocational class. On the contrary, it can be argued that the rigid format of the latter actually inhibits student involvement.

Table 2

Long classes in relation to total class provision (UK universities)

University	(a) Total	1979/80 (b) long classes	(b/a) %	(a) Total	1980/81 (b) long classes	(b/a) %
Hull	197	15	7·6	194	21	10·8
Keele	141	24	17·0	161	21	13·0
Leeds	227	91	40·0	215	96	44·7
London	793	343	43·3	836	117	14·0
Sheffield	229	22	9·6	229	12	5·2
Surrey	268	23	8·6	257	23	8·9
Others	6 329	71	1·1	6 637	85	1·2

Source: UCAE *Annual Reports*, 1979/80 and 1980/81, Table 3(a)

A related question is the degree to which the traditional image of the ideal adult education class affects the extent of the service offered by particular university extramural departments. The figures provided in Table 2 are revealing. The statistical returns make it clear that any ideological regard for the 'Great Tradition' is simply not reflected in the inventory of programmes for university departments in general. By the same token the claims still made on behalf of the ideal-type class are seen to be exaggerated. If the figures for the two major providers of tutorial and tutorial-type classes are excluded, then in the remaining thirty-five extramural departments only about 2% of total provision in 1979/80 was of long courses, and this attracted rather less than 2% of total enrolments. Tutorial classes in particular are, in the great majority of universities, a pronounced minority activity and this, it is argued, is indicative of the extent to which the importance of such classes is simply a myth which has taken its place in the folk-lore of adult education. The proportionate contribution of long courses is also plainly reducing year by year, and while some spokesmen for adult education continue to bask in the glow of the liberal tradition that particular contribution threatens to dwindle to vanishing point.

What is also strikingly obvious from Table 2, however, is that the traditional long-course policy has been preserved in the universities of

Leeds and London, and in attenuated form in several other institutions. Indeed the figures given seriously understate the dominance of long courses in those few departments still heavily committed to providing them. The totals of provision include 'continuing education' and other non-grant-aided work; therefore in the departments referred to the tutorial-type class is actually a much bigger proportion of conventional 'extramural' (that is, DES aided) provision than the raw figures suggest.

This survival has its implications also. Another challenge to the traditional myth is that long courses seem to have difficulty in satisfying even the minimum recruitment levels stipulated in the list of criteria. Clearly, as Jennifer Rogers points out, 'mere head counting is only the crudest measure of success in a class',[25] yet equally clearly head counting does have some place in the assessment of educational policies.

The statistics published by the Universities Council for 1980/81 show that 375 non-residential courses of three or more years' duration enrolled 6,341 students, and that there had been a marked decline from the session immediately preceding; average enrolment per class was 16·9 students. The bulk of these long-course enrolments continue to be accounted for by the universities of Leeds and London. Special circumstances have always affected adult education provision in the metropolitan area, and there average long-course enrolments in 1980/81 were 19·3 students per class. In Leeds the average for that session was 13·7. Such figures suggest that in general a decision to favour provision of long courses represents a very substantial allocation of increasingly scarce resources.

The final criticism which is put forward in the debate about the efficacy of tutorial-type classes moves away from the narrow issues of student numbers and academic standards. It is concerned with the broader question of whether adult education is orientated towards equality or excellence. The apparent dichotomous nature of this choice has always presented a fundamental dilemma, for the very notion of 'equality or excellence' implies incompatibility. This is made clear by June Purvis:

> On the one hand, it implies that the search for equality will mean a lowering of standards, a state of mediocrity. On the other hand, it implies that the quest for standards is a threat to equality.[26]

It is the effect of this apparent incompatibility which engenders criticism of the perpetuation in contemporary adult education work of the traditional class system. The class, it is argued, has little relevance to the needs of the majority of mature students. Its dominant ideology, based on a set of diffuse criteria which include curricula constraints, a specific institutional setting, outmoded teaching methods, egocentric teaching styles and inhibited social relationships, ensures that such a class continues to be unknown to the majority of adult students. The identification of the traditional liberal movement with a stratified form of knowledge suggests that its persistent preoccupation with a predominantly literary culture makes its work an alien experience to most adults. Its exclusion of applied and utilitarian subjects, its non-involvement with the physical and biological sciences and its denigration of a mass, hedonistic culture implies a preference for the study of selective and normative subjects associated with nineteenth century definitions of the cultured man.[27] The reality of the traditional class system therefore, it is argued, is that it provides an élitist, academic education for a self-selecting minority who have already profited from advantageous educational opportunities. More importantly, it completely ignores demands for compensatory education from the majority of the population.

The rejoinder

These five criticisms of the traditional class system rarely pass unanswered. The genuine commitment of many tutors and students in courses provided by the Responsible Bodies to the ethos of the system naturally produces a positive reaction to external destructive criticism. To these adults, the liberal adult education class is very much a reality and the counter-arguments which are advanced as a rejoinder to critics of the traditional class reflect this belief.

Adherence to regulations, it is sometimes contended, is a meaningless ritual which interferes with the true purposes of adult teaching. The common practice of admitting new students to the second and later years of established long courses is interpreted not as a following of the line of least resistance, but as a concomitant of that autonomy which allows the tutor to decide upon the value of the contribution which these students are likely to make to the work of an ongoing class.

In addition, the argument continues, the criteria of the ideal-type course as identified in this essay are historically limited and limiting. They are derived from a singular form of educational theory and practice, associated with a subject-centred curriculum and a scholastic tradition. The historical notion of the class presumes a belief in the linear and sequential development of knowledge and in an experience of education confined within the boundaries of 'subjects'. According to this outmoded view of adult learning, the unskilled student in the first year of an ideal-type class is gradually introduced to an ever-increasing complexity of knowledge and culture. Subsequently in each successive year, the maturing student is presented with new intellectual experience, the content of which he could not have coped with in earlier years.

The revisionist account of the special qualities of the adult class takes a different line. It argues that the traditional view of the perfect form of adult study overlooks an important educational fact — that in many subjects each year of a course is concerned with a specific topic area which is related to but not dependent on knowledge gained in previous years. Thus, a student who is recruited to a class in its second year will indeed have missed the study of such a topic, but this will neither prevent his full participation in the class nor will it devalue the worth of the work that is being done. Moreover, if it has to be accepted that the three year period is an essential component of the system, then this time clause can be satisfied in the 'revolving' course. Here a student who joins a class at any point in its existence will ultimately complete three years' membership, though he may have joined and finished at a later date than those students who enrolled at the initial inception of the course.

The second point of controversy is one which can be too readily over-looked. The issue at stake is the fundamental question of tutor autonomy. As a professional, the tutor has certain expectations about external and peer recognition of his expertise, commitment, responsibility and autonomy. Any insistence on the need to accept an institutional regulation is then seen as an infringement of professionalism unless the tutor has decided that, in his professional opinion, the regulation merits compliance. This type of reaction affects all professionals who work in organisations and its effects are well documented.[28] The central questions are who decides whether a class is a viable entity, or who decides whether new students may be admitted to an on-going class. Is it the tutor or is it the administrator? To these questions there are no universally agreed answers, for ultimately, the issue is whether a specific course can only be accepted by the administrator in terms of the listed criteria, or whether it is a satisfactory class when it satisfies the professional opinion of the academic evaluator.

The significance of this professional opinion is also noticeable in those counter arguments which are concerned with the issue of standards. Again, reaction to external criticism is complex. At one level the debate is concerned with the question of whether the evaluation of standards can ever be anything other than a subjective assessment. If this be so, it is argued, it is the tutor alone on the basis of his professionalism who can judge whether student activity satisfies the criterion which distinguishes the tutorial class from other less structured forms of educational activity. In turn, the interpretation of 'satisfies the criterion' or (in the words of the DES stipulation) of 'such written work as has been required', is dependent upon the tutor's professional conscience. This may lead the tutor to insist on the fortnightly essay, but he can equally well select some other form of written work to encourage the serious and systematic study of a subject. It is contended that the absence of an examination does not mean that the standards of a traditional liberal adult education class are low, for the examination is the example of subjective assessment *par excellence*, which contributes nothing to the development of study within the class.

At another level, the germinal issue is whether a minimal emphasis on written work, or indeed its total absence, necessarily destroys the claim of a course to its status as a real adult education class. The argument here is that written work should neither be seen as an end in itself nor be justified simply on the grounds that it is required by regulation. The critical question is whether it contributes to that goal of developing the serious and systematic study of a subject which is the basic reason for the existence of the class in the first place. Traditionally, the liberal studies class has been concerned with humanistic subjects and since it has been presumed that 'For the good of your soul it is necessary that you should study history, or literature and poetry',[29] then written work has been seen almost as a form of penance. But it is still the most suitable form of educational activity for the adult student? Does the completion of a piece or pieces of written work necessarily transform any established class into an accepted traditional class? The critic of the adult education class system claims that the class is a myth because of

21

the tendency to honour the regulation demanding written work more in the breach than in the observance. The traditionalist claims that the class is a reality when there is evidence of independent student effort, especially in the form of written work. This rejoinder argues that the issue of written work is subordinate in importance as a determinant of the merit of the class, to the more realistic criterion of the professional opinion of the tutor and that it is he and not an administrative regulation which must be satisfied if the class is to be a reality.

The third rejoinder which is put forward as an answer to criticism of the traditional class is less dependent on this intra-organisational notion of 'professional opinion'. Argument is based not on an inward looking preoccupation with standards but on an awareness of the relationship between the class and the demands of the community. Thus, in discussing the issue of minimum enrolments, it is argued that the class is indeed a reality, since, irrespective of the number of enrolments, it clearly satisfies students' needs. This rejoinder is based on the premise that the strength of the liberal adult education class lies in its unique ability to meet the most highly ranked of what has been termed 'the hierarchy of human needs'.[30] Other forms of adult education activity may be able to satisfy such lower-order needs on the ranking scale as those of survival, safety, social interaction and ego-satisfaction. Their provision of vocational classes, of classes which demand the minimum of intellectual activity or of courses which are admittedly recreational in character will thus attract large numbers of students. More rarely, courses can be mounted which meet the highest-ranked human need of self-fulfilment through encouraging creativity and self-realisation. But, it is claimed, only the traditional liberal studies class can meet fully these self-fulfilment needs. Indeed, it is more able than certificate, diploma and degree courses to achieve this, for the absence of examinations and the emphasis placed on a student-centred curriculum transforms the tutor and taught into a community of scholars who seek creativity and self-realisation.

The identification of the traditional class with the satisfaction of these higher-order human needs, constitutes a formidable argument in favour of the conclusion that such a class is a reality in adult education activity. It is an argument which is derived from a deeply held conviction that the curriculum of the course in conjunction with the experience of the adult, produces a class which is fluent, vital and organic. It is an argument, moreover, which has prestigious historical antecedents. From the very inception of the liberal adult education class, its supporters were fired by their belief in the ability of the class to meet the highest needs of man. Their spirit of comradeship in study and the belief of the students that learning was acquired not as a magpie picks up pretty bits of glass but as a means of raising themselves up and changing England, were indicators of how these classes were seen to meet specific human needs.[31] Repeatedly, the pioneers and visionaries of these early days, whether they were tutors or students, saw the traditional type of class as the great awakening which linked life and learning.

It is the legacy of this sense of spiritual emancipation which still encourages the supporters of the traditional class in their conviction that the class continues to be a reality, irrespective of the number of adult students who are enrolled. In the Tawney tradition they are opposed to begging people to join classes as if quantity made up for quality.[32] There is a continuing belief that the objective of meeting higher order human needs more than justifies the preference for a form of study which is attractive only to a minority audience. Yet this rejoinder cannot wholly answer critics of the traditional class who draw attention to its limited appeal, for this criticism is linked with the repeated comment that the paucity of student numbers is indicative of the extent to which adults do have needs that cannot be met by conventional class provision. In a sense, this point is the crux of the debate about the reality or myth of these classes. The advocate of the continuing merit of the established system of classes responds to this criticism in an argument, based on a limited interpretation of the role of adult education in meeting students' needs. Rightly or wrongly he argues that the ultimate goal of the traditional class, whether it be dependent on the belief that education is the means of social emancipation or on the conviction that students should have access to an otherwise élitist culture, must be identified with the perpetuation of academic excellence. Thus Tawney reacted to what he perceived to be the intellectual precociousness of the Marxist Social Democratic Federation; Mansbridge rejected the claims of Mactavish and his colleagues who saw education as primarily a weapon for the political advance of the workers.[33] Their successors have repeatedly divorced themselves from the demands of social engineering, even if this has meant that liberal adult education classes have become increasingly devoted to the provision of minority interest subjects. In short, the reality of the historic class, it is argued, is that it continues a long-standing tradition in adult education, the absence of which would seriously affect the perpetuation and development of intellectual and cultural activities.

Continuing controversies

The claim by supporters of the established class system that it has a unique and prestigious position in the hierarchy of educational provision consistently draws our attention to several specific areas of controversy. In the first of these, the fundamental issue is the structure and organisation of the traditional class, that is, there is considerable disagreement about the importance of specific teaching methods, the validity of the curriculum and also about the significance of established administrative regulations. Here, the attitudes of those supporters of the system who wish to maintain an historical tradition, can be contrasted with those of its critics who draw attention on the one hand to recent developments in educational technology and systems broadly understood, and on the other to the advantages of informal teaching in a less structured and non-institutionalised setting. Next, the related discussion about equality, excellence, social purpose considerably constrains objective assessment, for the apparent dichotomy which can be seen here is one that consistently modifies the identification and conceptualisation of these adult needs.

In contrast with the boundaries of these two areas which are limited to discussion of the structure of the traditional class *per se* the remaining two controversial issues are wider in scope. In the first of these, the critical question is that of the purpose of adult education. Discussion about the relationship of adult education to social change or about the function of adult education as a means of alleviating deprivation sees the conventionally structured class not as the ultimate form of educational activity, but simply as one way among many others of embodying the overall goals and objectives of adult education. Clearly, this does not of itself completely reject the worth of the traditional class. It is accepted that these classes can co-exist with other forms of provision, for their concern with academic humanities makes an important contribution to the transmission of culture. It is, however, clear from this discussion that the claim of supporters of the established class system to a special position at the apex of a hierarchy of educational provision is no longer secure.

Ultimately it can be inferred that the discussion about the myth or reality of the traditional class is effectively a debate about resource allocation. In this, the fourth and final area of controversy the basic issue is whether the diversion of funds to a minority activity can be justified in view of the competing claims of other activities. The Russell Report brings out clearly the financial needs of other than these classes in its review of university provision. Concomitantly, it draws attention to the claim of the WEA for support from public funds in the light of its role as an educational pioneer. The issue which then arouses controversy is whether the traditionally accepted status of the liberal adult education class means that it attracts financial support at the expense of other adult education activities. Reaction to this question again reflects individual interpretations of the purpose of adult education and it is clear that few assumptions can be made about the degree of consensus among tutors and taught.

These four areas of controversy thus illustrate the continuing debate in adult education not only about the merit of what is being done but also why it should be done. The specific question of the myth or reality of the traditional class is an important issue because of the prestigious status that has been claimed for this type of activity. But the importance of this particular issue goes beyond mere discussion of a specific type of provision. Its significance is that it is symptomatic of a wider concern for the rationalisation and rethinking of the use of limited resources in adult education and even though no readily attained solutions to encountered problems can be put forward, it suggests that traditional structures and methods will not necessarily be accepted without question. Thus the answer to the question of whether the traditional class is indeed a myth or a reality will be subjective and individual, but the answer will reflect an ongoing concern with what is a problematical idea of a need to meet the 'perceived educational needs' of adult students.

Education management

It is all too evident that in discussions about the future role of adult education the limitations identified by the evaluation of the effect of the liberal ethos upon contemporary university provision are but one part of a more general catalogue of constraining factors. Our second specific concern is thus with the consequences for the traditional pattern of liberal adult education programmes of introducing into this area the theory and techniques of *education management*. In the context of the traditional programme, 'management' has several meanings. At one level, it refers to a distinctive area of 'policy' or 'political' activities in this sector of education. The constituent parts of these activities have been carefully spelt out in a more general critique by Glatter. He identifies such factors as

> the relationships of power, influence and control between the various bodies and groups of participants within the educational system, and the way in which these relationships affect the policy process in the many areas of policy with which education is concerned. The term 'areas of policy' here would include both policy relating to particular stages of education, such as higher education, or pre-schooling, and also policy relating to particular categories of client, such as the handicapped or the adult illiterate.[34]

The implementation of the policy process has a significant effect upon the maintenance of the traditional pattern of provision, for at this macro-level, the relationships to which Glatter refers materially affect such critical factors as the allocation of resources. This is hopefully carried out with objectives of several different dimensions in mind. Adult educationists, for example, may simply and justifiably wish to see more value for money; that is, they are concerned with efficiency and cost-effectiveness. Alternatively, the need for efficiency and economy may be seen by them as part of a wider policy of priorities. With a 'no-growth' budget or with an expressed preference for the imposition of rigid cash limits upon budgets, development often necessitates the diversion of existing resources from what are claimed to be less essential or from inefficient elements in the pool of resources. In other words, the implementation of choice in the allocation of scarce resources will frequently result in the exercise of a policy of major redeployment. Alternatively, there may be ideological or political objectives which fall short of 'social engineering', but which reflect a belief that increased educational opportunity and the reduction of inequality of resources will materially improve the economic, social or intellectual well-being of the individual adult.[35]

In contrast, the subject we have come to know as education management is concerned at a second level with what Glatter terms

the internal operation of educational institutions, and also with their relationships with their environments, that is, the communities in which they are set, and with the governing structures to which they are formally responsible.[36]

In the context of providing liberal and non-vocational adult education courses, this aspect of management has had at this micro-level a considerable effect on provision. It has, for example, encouraged questions about the clarity of organisational purpose and practice. Since monitoring is impossible against unknown aims and objectives it has also encouraged debates about the certainty of organisational goals. It thus questions the tendency amongst supporters of the liberal tradition to evade, for a variety of diverse objective and subjective reasons, precise definitions of goals in the adult education sector.

At first, the distinction between the micro- and macro-level suggests a simple but very convenient dichotomy. It is an apparent distinction between *policy* and *management,* the boundaries of which were clearly spelt out by Sir Frederick Hooper, one of the early pioneers of the art and science of management in industry. He wrote in 1948:

It is the task of *policy* to lay down strategy; to assign objectives, establish priorities, and set the time scale. It is part of policy to lay down broad limits in money, manpower and resources generally, within which the programme must be carried through. It is the task of *management* to carry policy into effect with the fullest efficiency within the limits assigned; that is with maximum efficiency at minimum cost. It is the task of *management* to create conditions which will bring about the optimum use of all resources available to the undertaking in men, methods and material.[37]

Nevertheless, it would be highly misleading if this distinction were taken to imply a genuine conceptual dichotomy which differentiates issues of adult education policy and issues of adult education management.[38] What we are looking at in reality is an approach to adult education which is concerned with *both* the macro- and micro-levels and in which at the two levels, the utilisation of the theory and practice of educational management is *one* way of encouraging a critical evaluation of the maintenance in being of the traditional liberal studies programme.

The use of education management in this context has consequently to be analysed not only in terms of the extent to which it is a way of organising people within educational institutions but also in terms of the manner in which it refers to decision-making and resource allocation at government level. What we have to be wary of, therefore, are these perceptions of education management which in discussions of its relevance to the field of adult education favour too heavily either a macro- or micro-level approach. This is particularly so where the adoption of a specific choice suggests that we should favour one approach to the total exclusion of the other.

Objectives and 'prescriptive determinism'

What we would argue is that at both the macro- and micro-level, management approaches to the maintenance of the liberal-progressive movement are initially concerned with the common question of the goals of such a movement. In other words, the critical element of management in this context — particularly in the way in which it has affected the continuing provision of the traditional liberal programme — is identified with a persistent concern for aims and objectives. It is thus the existence of the latter and the concomitant stress placed on the essential need to check and constantly review administrative practices against stated educational intentions, which characterise the trend toward the utilisation of management theory and techniques in adult education.

One effect of this is very noticeable. A primary area of interest in this context is the two dichotomous views which we encounter about the real relevance of aims and objectives to the implementation of the traditional liberal studies programme. One point of view, for instance, questions our very ability to establish these aims and objectives. The rejection of their validity is rationalised on a number of grounds. It is, for example, argued that the objectives of adult education, like those of education in general, are too wide to be expressed in other than general terms. This argument reflects a thesis which is very clearly expressed in the views of Sir William Pile:

> On objectives I must confess to some scepticism. This is not so much about the value of a clearly stated objective as about the difficulty of expressing educational objectives in terms that are not as wide as a church door (for example, to improve the quality of education) or as narrow as the eye of a needle (for example, to ensure all childen can spell). Moreover my experience makes me cautious about the presumption that management textbooks seem to make that once an objective is clearly stated, specific policies can be squeezed out of it like toothpaste from a tube or will drip from it like whisky from a still. The real world does not seem to work like this.... So it seems that the formulation of an objective in generalized abstract terms and the selection of specific lines of action and policy rarely occur, in practice, as discreet phases but are usually inseparably entangled.[39]

The conclusion which we can apparently draw is that the objectives of adult education are so wide that we can neither readily nor easily establish precise aims and goals. Unidimensional models which seek to establish a clear determinant of policy — whether this be expressed in terms of rationality or that of instrumental change — become counter-productive since they usually fail to acknowledge that postulated rationality is derived from an ideal-type rather than from reality.

It can also be argued that it is difficult to identify the aims and objectives of adult education because educationists do not live in a static world. They live with uncertainties and the problems of reality — two features which are very much removed from the positivist's world of explicit and well-defined adult education objectives. Consequently, it is argued, the setting of the liberal adult education programme is one in which personality characteristics and value systems mould the pattern of provision and determine the shape of the provided curriculum. In this world, the ideology of non-ideology in liberal adult education cannot exist, for aims, it would seem, are in reality always the expression of values.

The emphasis, however, which is placed on the potential advantages for educationists of a static environment has to be treated with caution.

These advantages are clearly expressed by Webb when he argues that

> Creativity, freedom of professional expression, and opportunities to develop school relationships favourable to worthwhile learning are not inhibited by explicit and specific organization and planning but are given a stable context to operate in — and in education above all, this is surely vital.[40]

A completely different approach which has considerable implications for traditionalists in the area of adult education is provided, on the other hand, by Greenfield. He writes:

> In the conventional way of looking at organizations we resolutely split ends and means; we insist on thinking of organizations as means for the attainment of goals. This view fosters rational analysis of organizations; the goals provide criteria for assessing specific policies and practices and the organization itself. Such an approach lies at the base of programmed budgeting and management by objectives.

> Unfortunately these schemes assume a more rational world than actually exists, and so frequently fail. At least, they assume a different kind of rationality than usually prevails in the organizational world. In education, for example, we seem to think we need formal goals to define what goes on in schools. The assumption is that present activity is best understood not as an end in itself but as a means to an end, a means called into existence by some ultimate goal.[41]

A comment which also looks critically at the claims made for the advantages of aims and objectives is provided by Ormwell in his analysis of Bloom's *Taxonomy of Educational Objectives*. Ormwell concludes that

> One might describe the taxonomy... as being predisposed to fit a pragmatic, materialistic, meritocratic view of society in which few questions of value arise and in which explicit evaluation is always expected and preferred. These look uncannily like the assumptions of the old pre-crisis consensus in America. But they are hardly those implicit in either the oldest European concept of a 'liberal education' or in more recent radical theorizing about the 'social aims of education for life'.[42]

All these approaches, however, even if they differ in their conceptual and ideological standpoint, start from the premise that is it impossible to establish clearly-defined educational aims and objectives. The criticisms which we encounter all result from an underlying refusal to accept the validity of projected organisational models.

The alternative argument which reflects a second point of view is one which, notwithstanding these criticisms, begins from the premise that rational goals for adult education *can* be established. Considerable emphasis is placed on the advantages which can be gained in terms of course provision by exploiting a rational approach. This suggests in the first place that rational value-free management procedures are to be welcomed because their use leads to the more effective use of scarce and finite resources. More importantly, the efficacy of such procedures is seen to stem from the initial definition of the aims and objectives of the liberal adult education programme. Carried to a logical conclusion, the adoption of these procedures inexorably leads, it would seem, to 'maximisation'. This seemingly ensures that the provided service makes the best use of the resources which are allocated to it.

From this initial premise, which in itself is a negation of what Ormwell calls 'the European concept' of a liberal education, flows a tendency to accept uncritically the ideological and educational assumptions of stated goals and objectives. Carried to an extreme, this rejection of the highly contentious nature of educational aims becomes a basic characteristic of a management approach. Moreover, it encourages the growth within adult education of an educational *determinism* which ignores the extent to which the social frame of reference adopted by educational planners and decision-makers as a rationale of their proposals is a reflection of the subjective values to which we have referred. Determinism, in the context of traditional liberal adult education, supposes that in the framing of such a programme, decisions about curricula, course content and so on are made against a background of perfect rationality. By and large it refuses to recognise the persistence within educational decision-making of value-judgements. It is thus a rejection of that alternative point of view which argues that no one is altogether free from his context and upbringing, and that although rationality exists it cannot be disembodied or divorced from its context. This second point of view, in short, refuses to accept that decision-making is emotionally and institutionally invested like all other mental activity.

Educational determinism as a concomitant of management thus begins from the premise that the adopted rationality is value-free. In laying down future policy proposals, its proponents reject the argument that since both attitudes and values are at stake in all mechanical-structural changes in education, personal attitudes will inevitably come into play. Moreover, any attempt which is made to question the methodology or conceptual validity of 'value-free' is rejected — indeed any criticism of the objectivity of rational decisions is dismissed on the grounds of its irrelevance or irrationality. Educational determinism, in other words, either claims to be value-free or assumes that any criticism of the adopted value-system is personal, irrational and highly subjective.

In assuming that participants in adult education are passive rather than active instruments in future development, this management approach tends to be prescriptive in its recommendations. This is a trend which is a negation of much of the original philosophy which ensured that British liberal adult education in its formative years was both tolerant and cosmopolitan. Although the educational philosophies of pioneers such as Tawney and Mansbridge can be criticised at length,[43] their strength lay in the emphasis placed on individuality. Tawney sums this up very clearly:

> Our business, in my view is not to prescribe the lines which different individuals and groups should pursue, but to do our best, within our own field of non-vocational education, to meet their varying requirements, whatever these may be.[44]

Similarly, Mansbridge in commenting in 1912, on the University Tutorial Class stressed that 'its essential characteristic is freedom'.[45] This is not to deny that their successors have consistently exacerbated the inherent difficulties of this programme as educational management has sought to prescribe the process which individuals and groups *should* follow. There is a marked contrast here between claims for educational freedom on the one hand and management efficiency on the other. The latter in particular is a normative-based interpretation of educational purposes which can be rationalised in management terms in a number of ways. It can be claimed to facilitate the attainment of efficient administration. The key concept is the optimum or maximum utilisation of resources. This again stresses the point that decisions are thought to be based on the notion of the objective evaluation of alternative choices. Traditionally, the provision of liberal adult courses has exhibited as one of its major characteristics that spirit of voluntarism which has consistently motivated individuals. Such a spirit has engendered a complex set of identifying characteristics. This has been reflected, for example, in the manner in which the role of the teacher has been consistently equated not only with the possession of subject expertise but also with the display of commitment and responsibility towards the mature adult student. At the same time, both students and tutors have enjoyed a degree of autonomy which has enabled them to respond to perceived educational needs in the light of local circumstances. Such a response, moreover, has not been constrained by any reference to management efficiency. Prescriptive determinism, however, stresses the need for the more efficient and more effective use of resources. It thus contradicts the traditional set of attitudes, for this type of educational determinism is particularly opposed to the *laissez-faire* approach of much traditional-style adult education. It is concerned with rationality and cost-effectiveness. It suggests that at best the goals of adult education can be stated in terms of the measures and standards which are established by professionals employing rational knowledge.

In any case the emphasis is upon a structuralist approach to adult education. The aims of adult education, therefore, comprise two subsidiary objectives. In the first of these, the management system is related to such desired goals as those produced by educational planning based on a manpower requirements approach. The rationale of this approach is brought out clearly in the Venables Report on continuing education in the Open University:

> Judgements about priorities in the provision of courses must be informed not only by the educational and cultural aspirations of students, but also by the community's economic needs .... The possible advent of a national body in adult education could complement the Manpower Services Commission in terms of estimating the need for adult education of all kinds.[46]

We can infer from this statement that the goals of education management can be readily identified with the use of adult education resources as a kind of service industry for the national economy. A very real problem which then arises is that this is at variance with the traditional objectives of liberal adult education. The emphasis placed on 'the community's economic needs' contrasts markedly with declared intentions such as those of the 'Ontario Report', which stands against a schooled society based on a type of recurrent education which is support-ed in order to resolve the national employment problem and serve the national economy.[47] One critical question in the context of our discussion is whether supporters of the traditional objectives of British adult educa-tion can readily adapt their attitudes and accept the validity of objectives which are derived from a differing value-base.

The background to their problem, particularly in the way in which liberal adult education of the traditional variety has sought to rationalise its objectives is brought out very clearly by Ellwood:

> The Universities which were for the ruling classes would extend to the working classes the opportunity for personal liberation and cultiva-tion: technical colleges and night schools would provide the necessary vocational training for these people.[48]

What this indicates is that the liberal adult education tradition identified its objectives with a set of aims that were far removed from the more utilitarian concept of manpower planning strategies. This was a distinc-tion neatly summarised by Tawney when he wrote:

> one of the besetting sins of those in high places in England — it is not that of the working classes — is the the bad utilitarianism which thinks that the object of education is not education, but some external result, such as professional success or industrial leadership.[49]

The rationalisation of aims and objectives continues, therefore, to reflect a major contrast of purpose in which the instrumental objectives of the management approach to liberal adult education are diametrically opposed to the established belief that 'the liberal education of the worker is conceived as education for leisure'.[50]

The management approach, to stress the point, argues that in this context liberal adult education programmes in their traditional sense are outmoded because they are not able to respond to external demands for courses which are created on the basis of manpower planning strategies. The latter effectively produce aims and objectives which seek to establish a framework to control course provision and constrain curriculum choice. The determinist approach which argues in favour of the programme which should be adopted because it meets manpower goals thus contrasts markedly with an approach which concludes that 'the really important thing was that the university constitution should be sufficiently flexible to allow the university to play a full and creative part in leading and guiding the changing society around it'.[51]

The continuing difficulty is that the proponents of manpower planning strategies tend to forget that their rationalisation of ends and means is not value-free. As Doll comments: 'The rationality of clear ends and distinct means is really an *ex post facto* rationality; it is the result of a constraint man has placed on his completed actions'.[52] Consequently, while the proposals for the establishment of defined goals in adult education may seem to be perfectly rational to those who advocate them, other adult educationists will be decidedly critical of the arguments which are advanced. The latter have little sympathy for, or understanding of, an educational determinism which blandly assumes that its rationality alone represents a logical validation for the function and role of adult education within contemporary society. Inglis sums up this attitude very clearly:

> One style of thought which dominates curriculum and educational planning is directly a product of modern technocracies. It appeals to a model of reason whose terms derive from the coarse utilitarianism developed from the administration of social welfare in a mass competitive and consumer society. This model defines practical objectives and aims to calculate human response to them. Such models cannot ... answer tests of rationality but pass themselves off as rational because they answer the criteria of costs, productivity, growth and efficiency as defined by the input-output economists and investment accountants who uphold the system of planning in Whitehall and the corporations.[53]

Resources and 'opportunity cost'

This reference to issues of cost effectiveness and economic efficiency, draws our attention to the second of the objectives to which reference has been made. Whereas the first objectives relate the aims of the traditional liberal study programme to the issues of manpower planning strategies, the second objective is essentially concerned with 'the criteria of costs, productivity, growth and efficiency'.

It is therefore, the consideration of these which raises many of the truly critical questions about the future of the universities' activities in extramural education. The issue of cost, for instance, may encourage increasingly the demise of the traditional liberal programme. Conventionally, it has been readily assumed that the unit costs of liberal adult education courses are low. The calculation of these unit costs has been a relatively simple piece of arithmetic: total costs of expenditure for a given class have been divided by the total number of participants to give the average cost per student. An initial problem is whether the 'total costs of expenditure' have in fact been specified. Too frequently, as in the case of the calculation of the costs of the Open University, many 'real' costs have been overlooked. Increasingly, therefore, the emphasis which is placed on the advantages of introducing management techniques into the administration of adult education also bring into question the validity of these calculations.

The points which arise in this context are admirably summarised by Coombs and Hallack:

> The first truth is that any measure taken to improve educational quality or opportunity without prior examination of its cost consequences can easily prove self-defeating. The second truth is that, in most situations, costs have little meaning or value until they are set against educational results and the results weighed against the objectives. Costs, in other words, are only one side of the equation that links educational resource inputs to educational outputs and benefits. It is the equation as a whole — and this broader, more systematic way of looking at an educational process — that enables educational planners, evaluators and managers (broadly defined to include teachers) to improve efficiency and productivity of any educational activity.[54]

What this suggests is that evaluation of the efficacy of the traditional liberal studies programme has to move away from a simple assessment which is based on the singular notion of unit costs. Critical evaluation encouraged by the adoption of management principles is now increasingly concerned with attempts to get more and better education from the limited resources which are available. This accepts that 'cost analysis has no special magic to remedy faulty conditions'.[55] Nevertheless, education management emphasises that the basic advantage of cost analysis is to throw light on the relationship between resource inputs on the one hand and educational outputs on the other. This expands the area of interest very considerably. Unit costs based on a sensible choice of unit can illustrate relative expenditure. The true cost of providing the traditional liberal studies programme, however, is not simply the money that has to be paid out in terms of tutor fees, room hire, administration, postage, telephone calls and so on, less the income which is received. On the contrary, the true cost is the alternative way of using resources — the alternative opportunities — that have to be sacrificed when a particular choice is made. To the economist, the cost of the resources can be measured in financial terms such as expenditure or money value or in real terms — the time, for example, that is used to prepare a course programme. But no matter how these costs are measured, the fact which is now facing those who plan adult education courses is that when resources are devoted to one purpose or end, they are not available for alternative uses or activities.

Some of the practical implications of this conclusion have been clearly demonstrated in the *Annual Reports* of the Universities Council for Adult Education such as those of the 1970s. The *Report* for 1972/73, which came at a time dominated by the waiting for and the actual appearance of the Russell Report commented very forcefully on the relevance of liberal studies of the traditional kind. It noted that such programmes had been questioned *inter alia* by the then Chairman of the University Grants Committee, Sir Kenneth Berill, who in a speech at Birkbeck College in 1972 expressed the view that universities should not be involved in 'the bulk of adult education'.[56] Even so the *Report* did not really look at the opportunity costs of this pattern of provision, for its underlying purpose was to defend liberal adult education. Some indication of the problems that were likely to arise, however, appeared subsequently in the *Annual Report* for 1975/76, which welcomed the final report of a working party on Industrial Studies set up two years previously. The UCAE Council noted, however, that it had

> the difficult task of implementing the Report and trying, in a period of financial constraint, to obtain more resources to ensure that the research as well as the teaching of Industrial Studies by University Departments of Adult and Continuing Education can be intensified.[57]

The inference which could reasonably be drawn is that resources were so scarce at the time that no innovation could be countenanced. Yet, as the Council's own statistics show, there had been, and was to be, a continuing expansion of provision in the more traditional subjects of the liberal adult education programme.

Statistics of adult education provision are notoriously unreliable. Even so, the available figures do suggest that the preservation of a traditional liberal studies programme created substantial opportunity costs. Notwithstanding the recommendations of the *Report on Industrial Studies* and the subsequent deliberations of the UCAE Council, individual universities preferred to continue promoting their traditional programmes. The results for selected subject categories over four years from 1972 are shown in Table 3.

Table 3

Extramural provision by subject groups 1972 to 1976 (UK universities)

Subject group	1972/73	1973/74	1974/75	1975/76	1972 to 76 % change
Archaeology	640	696	684	724	+13·1%
Music	533	541	568	577	+8·3%
History	980	1 025	1 075	1 036	+5·7%
English Lang/Lit	853	869	875	893	+4·7%
Science	1 524	1 544	1 551	1 564	+2·6%
Economic/Ind Relations	618	583	620	533	−13·8%
All subjects	9 451	9 568	9 642	9 665	+2·3%

Source: UCAE *Annual Reports* 1972/73 to 75/76, Table 4

What we are looking at here is the result of resource allocation. Decisions in this context are not made by some *deus ex machina*. They are the expression of either conscious or unconscious preferences. Essentially, these are *political* decisions for they determine who gets what, when and in which amount. Although we can seek to rationalise on a variety of grounds the decisions which have been made, the reality is that, traditionally, decisions have been arrived at on the basis of a perception of adult education linked to the hierarchy of cultural legitimacy in the wider society. Within the context of liberal adult education provision, it is therefore possible to isolate certain trends. As Eileen

Byrne comments in the wider context of national educational resource allocation:

> By examining in retrospect how resources were actually allocated over a period of years and by then comparing practices with alleged objectives (or even alleged achievements), it has proved possible to trace certain recurrent patterns both nationally and locally, which I describe as an identifiable *rationale of resource allocation*.[58]

Similarly, for adult education in general and for the liberal studies programme in particular, we can see how, traditionally, provision was determined by the 'psychological or personal idiosyncracies of individual people who control or influence the budget or material resources'.[59]

Even if we do not wish to go so far as to attribute these characteristics to those whom Ellwood has called the 'professorial barons',[60] we can suggest that it is this exercise of choice that creates the opportunity costs to which reference has been made. Moreover, it is, we would argue, becoming increasingly evident that the established pattern of resource allocation which has hitherto underpinned and maintained the traditional liberal adult programme, is now subject to increasing criticism. We would also suggest that this criticism focuses on the opportunity costs of such a programme, and reinforces the claims of those who argue that only through the use of a management approach to course provision can effective adult education programmes be established.

The point which we would stress is that notwithstanding debates about the conceptual and methodological validity of education management *per se,* its concern with goals and objectives and its preoccupation with efficiency encourages critical evaluation of the traditional liberal studies programme. It questions *inter alia* what such a programme is trying to achieve. This is particularly so when macro-level national educational decisions are related to manpower planning strategies. More specifically, the increasing use of education management techniques and theories in the adult education sector raises repeatedly the question of opportunity costs. If the decision is taken to utilise scarce resources in one way, then this means that other types of provision have to be foregone.

Hitherto, such a decision has largely escaped scrutiny. On the one hand, the charismatic figures of adult education were able to plan and organise programmes of liberal studies without subjecting their choice to external evaluation. This expression of the personal wishes of those in charge was not necessarily wrong in principle. It did, however, create overall institutional patterns which reflected the preoccupations of the decision-maker and which chose to ignore the effects upon provision of the exercise of idiosyncratic choice. On the other hand, decisions often escaped critical assessment because the tools of evaluation were themselves suspect. The economics and management of adult education offer an area of analysis in which theory and praxis are still in a formative stage. Notwithstanding studies such as those of 'Costs and Potential Economies' in the university sector,[61] there has been considerable evidence hitherto of a reluctance to accept that it is possible to formulate methods for evaluating adult education requirements, resources and their costs. What we now suggest, however, is that increasingly such evaluation has to be carried out and that the conclusions arrived at will emphasise the extent to which the opportunity costs of the traditional liberal adult education programme make it difficult to justify the unchanged provision of such a programme.

On the other hand, decisions often escaped criticism because their rationale related to the perceived needs and wants of adult students. In particular, it was frequently argued that a given course of action was adopted precisely because it promised to meet students' needs. Keddie makes the point very clearly in commenting upon the report *A Strategy for the Basic Education of Adults,* when she writes of the report that it

> exemplifies the most extreme example we have seen so far of the way that a concept of individual need and student-centredness are used to legitimate an ideological commitment by adult education to the status quo. It makes it clear that needs are prescriptively defined by the educator in terms of the educator's perception of those needs, a perception which derives from a concept of disadvantage which seeks to remedy social problems through the imputed inadequacies of individuals.[62]

This raises a number of important issues in the context of the arguments put forward to justify the retention of the traditional liberal adult education programme, for it suggests that the rationale of these arguments goes beyond the logic of educational determinism. We need therefore to look more critically at the concept of needs and wants for it is clear that the identification of these has had a profound effect in the past on the construction of liberal studies provision. What we now have to question is whether this concept continues to affect materially the design of adult education programmes.

The future role

If the future of university extramural departments is no longer to be bound up solely with the continuance of the liberal non-vocational tradition, then the question of the future role of the departments has to be faced squarely. A popular stance is one that stresses the need for the university to develop its interest in *community education*. At face-value, this is a reasonable alternative to the dominance of the liberal tradition particularly where the object of community education is seen to be the need to break down barriers between the university and its immediate environment. An alternative role is one that identifies the university extramural departments more specifically with *education for participation* or with some form of *compensatory education*.

The continuing difficulty, which is inherent in all these answers however is that they do not necessarily make clear why universities are better placed than any other agency such as the WEA or the LEA, to work in those fields. Indeed, it can be argued that not only are other agencies better equipped with specifically trained staff but that there is a certain arrogance in the assumption of the university extramural departments that they can readily adapt to this projected role. Alternatively, it can be argued that the logical consequence of such a shift is an involvement with social engineering or community activism which ultimately replaces intellectual enquiry with polemical politics.

What is perhaps more disturbing is that much of the ongoing debate is expressed in terms of a zero-sum game; that is, the choice appears to be between liberal studies and community education or between compensatory education and non-vocational studies. To avoid this, I want to suggest that the answer to the persistent question of the future role of universities lies in the pioneering work carried out by leaders of the Extension movement within universities in the last quarter of the

41

nineteenth century. Their aim, of an open-door university designed to meet the needs of those who sought a new definition of a university career, continues to be a purpose the satisfaction of which justifies the maintenance in being of university extramural departments. It is an objective which suggests that the universities should provide a serious form of adult education without special regard for the social condition of students or for satisfaction of political aims. Rather, the aim of extramural departments should be to seek to provide part-time adult students with access to the whole range of teaching and research which the university provides for the school leaver.

In many ways this explains the importance of *continuing education* in stating the obvious, but in the light of claims made for a shift of university adult education resources to other non-traditional and inno-vatory areas, it is, I feel, necessary to restate the obvious. The role of the university department of extramural studies is to facilitate the access of the public to university education and university research. It is a tradition which has a notable pedigree. As Marriott observes:

> There has been too much loose talk and writing about a 'Great Tradition' in English adult education. The tradition is older and more complex than the 1919 Report or the adaptations that have subse-quently been made of its philosophy. Our perceptions of the present might be enriched if we recognised the longer tradition.[63]

To implement the tradition, universities will be again obliged to look more critically at the interests of the public particularly in terms of access to degrees and diplomas. But paradoxically, departments of extramural studies will have to be correspondingly more inward looking. The 1919 Report spawned extramural departments which to many members of the university were the WEA at work or academics at play. The marginal status attributed to organised adult education in many universities was thus both a cause and effect of the over-willingness of some university tutors to identify with outside agencies rather than with their own institutions. Now, the time has come for these extramural departments to stress that they are that part of the university which has the experience and the expertise to work in association with internal departments in the joint provision of university-standard courses for the public.

This is the future role and function of university extramural departments. It will be challenged by many who prefer to identify adult education with social engineering. It will be questioned by those who are scornful of university 'standards'. It will be disliked by tutors to whom the university is little more than a distant paymaster. It is a role, however, which recognises the opportunities that exist to bring to the community the full range of university teaching and research free from continuing debates about social purpose, or about the non-vocational purpose of adult education, or about the 'right' length of a course. It is a role above all which would lay down a curriculum of study 'on new lines suited to the needs of those who desire to carry on their intellectual culture side by side with the regular business of life'.[64] Hitherto, we have seen a pattern of extramural provision deliberately designed to further what in England and Wales is seen as *Adult Education*. Now the time has come for the development of the *education of adults* within a programme framework which recognises the potential worth of the contribution which universities can make on the basis of their teaching and research expertise. There is, however, a very real danger that extramural departments will seek to continue their preference for providing general courses within the framework of the liberal tradition and that they will leave to others the responsibility for providing strong continuing professional education, role education and renovative education. To avoid this danger, university extramural departments must respond to the challenge of the coming decades and ensure a comprehensive approach which utilises the wealth of the *university* in providing for the *education of adults*.[65]

Notes and references

1. British Institute of Adult Education and the Tutors' Association *The Tutor in Adult Education: an enquiry into the problems of supply and training* (Dunfermline: The Carnegie United Kingdom Trustees, 1928), p. 19.

2. Ministry of Reconstruction, Adult Education Committee *Final Report* Cmd 321 (HMSO, 1919), p. 5. The '1919 Report' as it is commonly termed has been reprinted with introductory essays by H. Wiltshire, J. Taylor and B. Jennings as *The 1919 Report* (Nottingham University, Department of Adult Education, 1980).

3. Thomas Kelly 'Two reports: 1919 and 1973' *Studies in Adult Education* 5, (1973), p. 118.

4. Rex Warner 'Education' in C. Day Lewis (ed) *The Mind in Chains* (Frederick Müller, 1937), p. 26.

5. For a further examination of this point see J. E. Thomas and G. Harries-Jenkins 'Adult education and social change' *Studies in Adult Education* 7, (1975), pp. 1–15.

6. Thomas Kelly *A History of Adult Education in Great Britain* (Liverpool: the University Press, 1970), p. 237.

7. June Purvis 'Equality and excellence in adult education' *Studies in Adult Education* 5, (1973), p. 157.

8. T. S. Eliot *Essays Ancient and Modern* (Methuen, 1949), pp. 3–4.

9. R. W. Livingstone, *Greek Ideas and Modern Life* (Oxford: the University Press, 1935), p. 115.

10. Flann Campbell 'Latin and the élite tradition in education' *British Journal of Sociology* 19, (1968), pp. 308–25.

11. Ministry of Reconstruction *Interim Report of the Committee on Adult Education* Cd 9107 (HMSO, 1918), para. 2.

12. Keith Jackson in Foreword to Jane L. Thompson (ed) *Adult Education for a Change* (Hutchinson, 1980), p. 10.

13. Rex Warner 'Education', pp. 27–28.

14. *Final Report,* p. 171.

15. Caroline Ellwood *Adult Learning Today* (Sage, 1976), p. 39.

16. S. G. Raybould *Twenty-one Years of Adult Education — 1946–67* (Leeds University, Department of Adult Education and Extramural Studies, 1967), pp. 5–6. See also the same author's *University Extramural Education in England 1945–62* (Michael Joseph, 1964), especially pp. 185–6.

17. John Lowe *Adult Education in England and Wales* (Michael Joseph, 1970), p. 106.

18. Oxford University, Joint Committee of University and Working-class Representatives *Oxford and Working-class Education* (Oxford: the University Press, 1908), pp. 47–8.

19. Bernard Jennings *Albert Mansbridge* (University of Leeds, 1973), p. 4.

20. Bernice Martin 'The mining of the ivory tower' *Times Higher Education Supplement,* 18 April 1975, p. 7.

21. Roy Shaw in Editorial Introduction to Universities Council for Adult Education *Annual Report 1973–74,* pp. 3–12.

22. Shaw, p. 11.

23. R. H. Tawney to A. Mansbridge, 30 March 1909 (Rewley House MSS, Oxford University, Department for External Studies).

24. Albert Mansbridge *The Kingdom of the Mind* (Meridian Press, 1946), p. 25.

25. Jennifer Rogers *Adults Learning* (Harmondsworth: Penguin Books, 1971).

26. J. Purvis 'Equality and excellence', p. 145.

27. Purvis, p. 155.

28. G. Harries-Jenkins 'Professionals in organizations' in J. A. Jackson (ed) *Professions and Professionalization* (Cambridge: the University Press, 1970), pp. 53–107.

29. Mansbridge *Kingdom of the Mind,* p. 67.

30. Abraham Maslow *Motivation and Personality* (New York: Harper and Row, 1970).

31. J. E. Henighan to A. Mansbridge, 2 February 1908, cited in Ross Terrill *R. H. Tawney and his Times* (Andre Deutsch, 1974), p. 41.

32. R. H. Tawney to S. G. Raybould, 29 September 1948, cited in Terrill, p. 100.

33. Mary Stocks *The Workers' Educational Association* (Allen and Unwin, 1953), p. 40.

34. R. Glatter *Influence or Control? A Review of the Course,* E.222, Unit 16 (Milton Keynes: Open University Press, 1979), Section 5.2.

35. For a fuller discussion of this point, particularly in relation to resource allocation in British local education authorities, see Eileen M. Byrne *The Rationale of Resource Allocation,* E.321, Unit 16 (Milton Keynes: Open University Press, 1976), pp. 13ff.

36. Glatter *Influence or Control?,* Section 5.3.

37. Frederick Hooper *Management Survey* (Harmondsworth: Penguin Books, 1948), p. 11.

38. R. Glatter, 'Education "Policy" and "Management": one field or two?' in G. Fowler (ed) *Educational Analysis* (Falmer Press, 1979), Chapter 1.2.

39. Sir William Pile 'Corporate planning for education in the Department of Education and Science' *Public Administration* 52, (1974), p. 18.

40. P. C. Webb 'Staff development in large secondary schools' *Educational Administration Bulletin* 2, (1973), p. 24.

41. T. B. Greenfield 'Organizations as social inventions: rethinking assumptions about change' *Journal of Applied Behavioural Science* 9, (1973), pp. 551–74.

42. C. P. Ormwell 'Bloom's Taxonomy and the objectives of education' *Education Research* (November 1974), pp. 4–5. Ormwell refers to B. S. Bloom (ed) *A Taxonomy of Educational Objectives. Handbook* I: *Cognitive Domain* (New York: David McKay Co., 1956).

43. See for example M. Stephens and G. Roderick 'Adult education and the community university' *Adult Education* 45, (1972), p. 142.

44. R. H. Tawney 'The WEA and adult education' in Rita Hinden (ed) *The Radical Tradition* (Harmondsworth: Penguin Books, 1964), p. 90.

45. Mansbridge *Kingdom of the Mind,* p. 24.

46. The Open University *Report of the Committee on Continuing Education* (Milton Keynes: The Open University, 1976), pp. 26–27.

47. Report of the Commission on Post-secondary Education in Ontario *The Learning Society* (Ontario, 1973).

48. Ellwood *Adult Learning Today,* p. 48.

49. R. H. Tawney 'An experiment in democratic education' in *The Radical Tradition,* p. 85.

50. Eric Robinson *The New Polytechnics* (Harmondsworth: Penguin Books, 1968), p. 15.

51. University of Birmingham *Report of the Review Body appointed by the Council* (21 September 1972), p. 7.

52. W. E. Doll 'A methodology of experience: an alternative to behavioural objectives' *Educational Theory* 22, (1972), p. 309.

53. F. Inglis 'Ideology and the curriculum: value assumptions of systems builders' *Journal of Curriculum Studies* 66, (1974), p. 1.

54. P. H. Coombs and J. Hallak *Managing Educational Costs* (New York: Oxford University Press, 1972), p. xi.

55. Coombs and Hallak, p. x.

56. Universities Council for Adult Education *Annual Report 1972–73,* p. 4.

57. UCAE *Annual Report 1975–76,* p. 3.

58. Eileen M. Byrne *The Rationale of Resource Allocation*, p. 7.

59. Ibid.

60. Ellwood *Adult Learning Today*, p. 236.

61. J. A. Bottomley *Studies in Institutional Management in Higher Education: the University of Bradford, costs and potential economies* (Paris: OECD, 1972).

62. Nell Keddie 'An ideology of individualism' in J. L. Thompson (ed) *Adult Education for a Change*, p. 62. The reference is to the Advisory Council for Adult and Continuing Education report *A Strategy for the Basic Education of Adults.*

63. Stuart Marriott *A Backstairs to a Degree: demands for an open university in late Victorian England* (Leeds University, Leeds Studies in Adult and Continuing Education, 1981), pp. 96–7.

64. *University Extension Journal* (February 1891), p. 3, quoted in Marriott *A Backstairs*, p. 1.

65. Paul Fordham 'Continuing to falter' (Southampton University, Department of Adult Education, 1982, duplicated).

Does university adult education in Britain have a future?

Alastair D. Crombie

Introduction

It is generally acknowledged that in the field of adult education British universities have a distinctive, and distinguished past. In a number of cases, where local colleges which had been used for extension lectures were turned into universities, adult education played a major part in their very origins. As Professor Kelly puts it in his authoritative history: 'The most distinctive feature of adult education in this country in modern times has been the contribution of the universities'.[1] In its hundred year history since the inauguration of extension lectures by the University of Cambridge in 1873, its contribution has been to legitimate the education of adults as a worthy social concern, to elevate its intellectual aspirations, and to promote a very wholesome interaction between universities and their local communities.

It is today coming to be acknowledged with equal generality that adult education stands on the threshold of a renaissance, global in its scale. From countries around the world, east and west, over-developed and under-developed, capitalist and socialist, come signs of a new bouyancy and optimism in adult education — a feeling that education for adults is at last (and one should perhaps add, at least) firmly on the policy agenda. In the industrialised world this renaissance is due to the societal transformations wrought by science and technology since the Second World War, and a growing public awareness that today's child will survive into a world quite different from that of his birth, and will therefore need to be educationally equipped for it. In the 'third world' it is due to the urgency that now attaches to development on this shrinking planet, and the imperative of mass literacy for such projects, as an instrument for further learning of every kind. To be in adult education today is to live in exciting times.

In the light of these observations it might be thought absurd to throw any doubt on the future vitality of university adult education in Britain, and yet the question posed in the title is not intended to be entirely rhetorical. In times of rapid change and sweeping transformations, an illustrious past is no guarantee of a secure future, and may even become an impediment when basic assumptions need to be re-examined. This is as true for the universities themselves as it is for their extramural or adult education departments of course. Already over the past decade or so a number of major policy initiatives in higher education — the establishment of the polytechnics, the introduction of CNAA degrees, and the founding of the Open University — have been designed in part to overcome or circumvent the reluctance of the universities to change themselves, with the result that the universities are now an *element* within a higher education system, rather than synonymous with it. If university adult education were to fail to meet its novel challenges and responsibilities, it would be possible for the paymaster to expand the mission of the public sector, and leave the universities to their own devices.

I believe that a future for university adult education ought not, and indeed cannot be taken for granted, and that as a corollary an active, wide-ranging search for possible and desirable alternative futures should become a priority task for university adult educators. The problem can be simply stated. The basic axioms and ideals of university adult education were distilled out of the socio-economic context of the late nineteenth and early twentieth centuries, when education was essentially scarce but optimism concerning its potential abundant, when religious experience still held more mystique than did technology, and the printed word was the only medium of mass communication. This socio-economic context has been transformed beyond imagination. Today, formal education is not only relatively abundant but for eleven years compulsory, and yet the just and plentiful society seems if anything further afield, and there is a growing feeling that public investment in 'schooling' has produced diminishing returns.

The original axioms and ideals have not remained completely untouched by the passage of time, yet in their emphasis on the timeless and universal worth of guided intellectual enquiry as the road to personal development and civic maturity, they embody a strong conservative tendency, and this I believe is proving inhibitive of the new 'appreciations' that are so needed.[2] University adult education can thus be observed from time to time in the throes of 'dynamic conservatism' — fighting to remain the same, in a radically different world. This problem of anchorage to the past is compounded by the fact that out of the more recent socio-economic context have grown an impressive range of *new* institutions with an interest in adult and continuing education, free of any such constraints, and better equipped in many respects to respond to the challenges ahead. Before going on to identify these new organisations and evaluate their potential, I would like to explain the perspective from which this critique is constructed, and to preview its major themes.

First, my perspective is bound to have a comparative dimension, as my own experience in university adult education has been gained since 1973 as a member of the Centre for Continuing Education at the Australian National University in Canberra. I first came to Australia in 1969 to complete my training as a sociologist, and in the course of my doctoral research came to realise that what most interested me was the application of behavioural science to social problems and social change. In exploring what this might mean in practice, I found both friends and opportunities at the Centre for Continuing Education, under the Directorship of Chris Duke, who had also arrived in Australia in 1969, from the University of Leeds. I participated in and contributed to the Centre's conferences on group dynamics and the development of human resources, and did some teaching in the area of my speciality. After completing my doctorate and spending a year back in England I returned to Australia to the post I still occupy, turning from the somewhat sterile prospect of a career as an academic sociologist to the challenge and stimulation of the theory and practice of continuing education. It was, therefore, as a sociologist, in Australia, in the early 1970s that my acculturation in adult education began, and it has always been the distinctive threats and opportunities of the current 'world problematique' that have dominated my own struggles with the question 'What should adult education do?'

To put it another way, this acculturation was somewhat innocent of the great debates and struggles, heroes and scoundrels, triumphs and defeats that are the stuff the past is made of. This was not for lack of curiosity or respect for the history of our movement, which I have over the years gradually come to understand and appreciate more fully. It rather reflected the fact that ours was a new enterprise, in a new city, in a young and dynamic country, and that the future filled our vision. While there are in Australian adult education those who began the march long before I was born, and who were stirred by ideals of equality, liberalism, civic maturity, and a quest for the kind of unalloyed truth that reason was once held to produce, they are somewhat thin on the ground, and have always seemed to me to have an expatriate rather than a distinctively Australian orientation.

Suffice it to say that in Canberra there were few with whom the past could be shared, and it was the prospectus of Toffler rather than Tawney that seemed to pose the kind of questions that adult education should be attending to in the 1970s. The role for the professional in continuing education that has evolved in our practice reflects in part the role adopted for the Centre as a 'look-out institution'.[3] The task of such an institution includes 'future-scanning', and seeking to identify those parts of the social fabric in which new conflicts and challenges are emerging, so as to find co-operative and participative means by which these problems might be more adequately defined, understood, and responded to. For the academic staff this work has consistently led in the direction of educational consultancy and action-research rather than the preparation of course programmes and teaching of classes, although these kinds of work are by no means eschewed.

Nevertheless, just as Australian universities as such derive essentially from the British tradition, so university adult education owes most of its basic structure and assumptions to British practice and custom of one sort or another. As elsewhere in the Commonwealth therefore, one is working within a field whose history, when it is evoked, does trace back to nineteenth century Britain, and which looks with particular interest at the latest developments there. During 1979 I was able substantially to extend and deepen my understanding of the character of adult education in British universities by virtue of a six month visiting fellowship in the Department of Adult Education at the University of Nottingham. During this time I visited fifteen other departments or centres, attended four major adult education conferences, visited and had discussions with some of the staff of the National Institute of Adult Education (NIAE), the Advisory Council for Adult and Continuing Education (ACACE), and the Open University, and generally immersed myself in the university adult education scene.

The first draft of this paper was completed in England, where it was judged stimulating by some, but scurrilous by others who might have published it. Since returning to Australia at the end of this period of study leave, my initial status as an expert on the state of British adult education has dwindled to nought, yet my awareness of and interest in the issues and events that have preoccupied it have I believe been better informed. Several recent monographs, the journals, the most valuable publications which emanate from the NIAE and ACACE in particular, and the professional exchange made possible by the Commonwealth Relations Trust have all helped to enrich and update the impressions formed and information collected in 1979. This then is the context of experience and training from which I have sought to raise some worthwhile questions about the future of British university adult education. I hope the reader will be kind enough to grant that there are some strengths to balance its obvious weaknesses.

It is perhaps worth noting in addition, that since most of the drafting of this paper took place, adult education in Australian universities has been having a very severe time of it. At Sydney University, once the flagship of the fleet, where tutorial classes have been run in association with the WEA since 1913, the retirement of a long-standing Director has been seized as the occasion to abolish the Department as an academic entity. A high-level external committee of review has just made essentially the same recommendation to the University of Adelaide, the pioneer institution in South Australia, which first offered tutorial classes in 1917. The University of Melbourne has already closed down its short-lived Office of Continuing Education, an exciting pre-recession initiative, while there is a review in progress at the University of Western Australia that seems unlikely to come to any happier conclusions. This is going on in the midst of a gathering consensus amongst policy-makers, thinking people, politicians and the media alike, that Australia's climb out of the presently deepening recession will have to be in the direction of information and knowledge-based industries for which the key factor of production is human capital.

The more pertinent context is of course the severe financial constraints imposed on higher education by government, and adult education's lack of political favour and support, either within university power structures or within society as a whole. Something of a pattern is emerging: growing pressure on university resources motivates a hunt for any 'non-essential' parts or activities; adult education's perennial marginality and its quiet growth during the good years of the sixties gave it an almost luminiferous appeal; a heavyweight review committee is established, notably bereft of recognised authorities on adult education, to take a 'fresh look' at its role in the university; our colleagues in the teaching departments (where the 'essential business' of the university is carried on) and the pragmatists who prepare and administer the budgets sigh with regret as they slip the knife in.

These antipodean tales must of course be held in the correct perspective. One would hesitate to extrapolate from the fates of these Australian departments to what might happen in British universities. One is aware nevertheless of a financial squeeze in higher education in Britain, and my own impression has been that adult education is not much more of a vote-winner in the Mother Country than it has been Down Under.

To return now to the development in British adult education of the past ten years or so, it is striking to see how much the field has been changed, and will continue to change as a result of initiatives already taken and others yet to come. Despite its own somewhat precarious existence from its creation in 1977, the Advisory Council for Adult and Continuing Education did, with notable purpose and vigour, seize the initiative in relation to policy development, a leadership of progressive and creative thought eventually consolidated in the Council's proposals for the development of a continuing education system in England and Wales for the next twenty years.[4] Together with its earlier reports and discussion papers this major step towards national policy making is likely to set the parameters for debate and planning within adult education for the next decade. ACACE has not of course been in competition with the universities, which were indeed well represented on it, but it sought to fill the vacuum of national leadership in adult education, a role that university adult educators might well have taken up, and to which they may yet be able to make a richer contribution.

Two other fledgling organisations, the Manpower Services Commission (MSC) and the Open University, have come pouring down the flanks in the past two years, and now occupy substantial territory in the education of adults. In the response of the universities one can detect measures of bemusement and irritation, and occasionally outright resentment. In conversation about the Open University for example one Director assured me that the money would have been better spent by parcelling it out amongst the existing extramural departments.

The MSC, through its Training Services and Special Programs Division, which together account for expenditure in excess of half a billion pounds, has become a major force in the field of vocational training and education. Due in some measure to the persistence of the inept distinction between vocational and non-vocational education, and to the inability of the local authorities to guarantee delivery of the training programmes required, this vast investment in continuing education is administered via the Department of Employment. As the first ACACE Discussion Paper observed:

> What is particularly striking about the vocational sector is that much of the initiative and finance for its recent development has come from employers, trade unions and industrial agencies such as the Manpower Services Commission and the Industrial Training Boards rather than the public education sector.[5]

As befits such a professional and ambitious agency the MSC has adopted an expansive conception of its purpose that calls out for partnership with the education system, to enable the country's manpower resources to be developed and contribute fully to economic well-being; and to ensure that there are available to each worker the opportunities and services he or she needs in order to lead a satisfying working life. Yet even while lauding the strategy of recurrent education or lifelong learning, the universities have rather turned their backs on these merely vocational pursuits, and there is little evidence of either a theoretical or a practical sort of attempt to nurture the kind of integration between labour market and educational policies that the MSC and the theorists of recurrent education are seeking.

In the area of initial vocational training as opposed to retraining the Business Education Council (BEC) and the Technician Education Council (TEC), again both of recent origin, have set about the task of rationalising and upgrading provision in this area, and are producing a novel blend of multi-disciplinarity, theory and practice from which adult educators may yet have something to learn.

While the Open University has pioneered most substantially in the areas of open-access, part-time degree study, and the use of broadcasting media, it has also set the pace in its advocacy and introduction of credit transfer arrangements, and shown a lead in the vital area of advisory and counselling services for mature-age learners. Using its distinctive pattern of part-time, distance education the OU now has around 58,000 graduates (1981 figures), a current student body of nearly 87,000 of which a large and growing proportion are Associate Students and others, registered for shorter, post-experience courses or community education courses. It seems likely that the further development of the Associate Student programme and of its community education and 'adult concern' courses will come to represent an increasingly attractive option to those in the traditional adult education markets. It is disturbing to find senior university adult educators who are still resentful of the very existence of the OU, or threatened by the progress it is making with its non-degree work. The OU defines all of its work as continuing education.

In the LEA sector, while the adult course provision has been the first and hardest hit by Government stringencies, it is apparent that many of the polytechnics are aiming at vigorous growth in the areas of post-experience and continuing professional education, and that they are going about this in a business-like way. While their capacity to do so relates in good part to the saleability of their goods, they are aided, one suspects, by freedom from the scruples that keep the majority of their university colleagues (if this is the right term) comfortably insulated from the burgeoning sphere of fee-for-service education. This entrepreneurial approach to post school education is becoming more evident within the business and commercial sector itself, fulfilling that basic postulate of the dismal science that where a demand comes into existence a supply will be called forth. As the spectrum of such provision broadens from the traditional lines of languages, crafts, driving, cookery and the like into a much more substantial and diverse offering of vocational, professional, and personal development courses, it will be important to have a body of professional adult educators who are sufficiently in touch with this learning market, and sufficiently respected by its managers to be able to exert an influence in a positive direction over the quality of the educational processes used and the calibre of the teachers.

My purpose here is not to make a comprehensive review of current developments in adult education, but rather to support the impression that I have formed of the wise old centenarian, university adult education, being crowded off its favourite perch by a bevy of brash young competitors for the hearts, minds, and money of the adult learner. The old bird certainly has been around for a long time, and still has some handsome plumage, but is it immortal?[6]

Suffice it to say that 'the world waits for no man'. It is beyond question that we live in a time of fundamental transformation and great challenge in the affairs of humankind. The acceleration of the rate of change itself has become the predominant characteristic of our times. Traditions great and small need to be reassessed against the turbulence ahead, and we will need to work harder at identifying and articulating our concepts of a desirable future, and the values implicit in these. I believe that, within this context, it has become urgent for university adult education to begin an active search for its role in the future — a search which must take full account of the 'distinctive competence' of the university itself, as well as new developments in adult education of the kind described above, and which will oblige us as adult educators to undertake more systematic and serious analysis of the sort of world that we are moving into, and above all, of the sort of world we desire, and would help to produce.

In his inaugural lecture at the University of Hull in 1975, Professor Bernard Jennings made the following observations by way of introduction: 'University adult education is just over a hundred years old. There have been three main structural developments during this period, the inauguration of extension lectures in 1873, the launching of tutorial classes in 1908, and the establishment of university departments of adult education at differing dates from 1920'.[7] My argument will be that a fourth is overdue. If there is to be a future for university adult education, other than the residue that will remain when ACACE, the Open University and the Manpower Services Commission have blazed their trails, and the local authorities again have money to spend on a coherent and comprehensive adult provision, then university adult education will have to become proactive, and set about determining what it is that the university departments will be able to do distinctively well in the 1990s. What are the dimensions along which university adult education might have to change in order to become a leading part in a revitalised adult education movement?

Twenty-six universities in England and Wales have Departments (or Centres) of Adult Education, Extramural Studies, or Continuing Education, which conduct courses for the liberal education of adults, and twelve of these have a further commitment to teaching and research in the subject of adult education. I am not sure myself whether the panoply of nomenclature worn by these entities is a sign of robust diversity or mere confusion, but I suspect that the fashions are worth studying. In generalising about these twenty-six under the collective term 'university adult education' one is asserting the existence of some common or typifying characteristics, and it will be as well to acknowledge at the outset some awareness of the great differences that are also to be found. While an empirical study would have to pay much more attention to these, my purpose is to explore the basic assumptions and principles which, because they are part of the history and development of the movement, have influenced the whole enterprise of university-based adult education. It is these general assumptions and principles which give meaning to claims by individual institutions to being 'different' or 'innovative', and against them, therefore, that such claims have to be evaluated.

Psychoanalysis has helped us to appreciate the way in which underlying beliefs, fears and commitments — the psychic axioms at the core of the personality — will issue in patterned behaviour and interactions despite a lack of awareness, or even denial of their existence. It is generally agreed that gaining insight into these deep-seated assumptions is most helpful to healthy growth and development. Organisational analysis reveals a similar structure. An organisation gains coherence and integrity from the embodiment of values and ideals which constitute the core of the organisational culture. These 'axial principles' are invariably played out in the organisation's structure and functioning — its behaviour and interactions with its environment — even where consciousness of them is slight, or they have entirely ossified. (In such cases of course we would anticipate some organisational pathology, and be inclined to look for some new leadership to revitalise a sense of direction and purpose.)[8] I believe that there are such axial principles underlying the enterprise of university adult education, however attenuated they may have become in certain corners of the fold. They derive from a common origin, from the philosophies and beliefs of its distinguished leaders, from the precepts which have been built into its legislative and financial framework, and from the lore of its battles and celebrations.

After exploration of this fundamental dimension, the analysis turns to each of the three levels at which, and between which, one sees or fails to see these principles and assumptions in purposeful activities: the level of the university itself, of the whole of which university adult education is but a part; the level of the functions and roles that are allocated to its professional members; and the level of the department or centre itself, at which choices have to be made about both internal structures and processes, and external relationships. Productivity and effectiveness in the long run require that these three levels be well integrated around a set of axial principles which seem to be relevant to future environments as well as to past ones, and from which meaningful roles and functions can be derived.

Beyond the tradition

The 'Great Tradition'

li'beral a.&n. **1.** Fit for a gentleman (now rare exc. in -*education*, i.e. directed to general enlargement of mind, not professional or technical)[9]

The state of mind which prevails in extra-mural departments ... has its roots in a cult of non-vocational courses, a feeling of inferiority in relation to internal departments, and a literature full of folk heroes advocating narrow and often misguided philosophies.[10]

When one searches for the axial principles of university adult education, the path leads back to the set of ideas and values enunciated by Harold Wiltshire in 1956 as the 'Great Tradition', even though it was his own view at the time that this was a dying tradition, and the forces that he identified as threatening this tradition have not abated. Contemplating these changes in 1956, Wiltshire concluded that 'this is a mere assemblage of new ventures, that has everything except purpose and conviction', and went on to ask whether the great tradition could yet inform and inspire the new developments. This 'great tradition', he wrote, merits its name:

for it is the central one which has inspired many generations of teachers and students, it has made adult education a movement as well as a service and it alone has been able to give adult education purposes and principles which have made it more than the mere

59

'pis aller', the substitute for a 'proper' university education which it would otherwise have been.[11]

The fact that this is still the essence of the British approach becomes clearer when, as seems to be a common occurrence these days, it is put in an international perspective, so that comparisons can be drawn in particular with the North American and European traditions. While such contrasts are still readily identifiable of course, there is no doubt that they were more striking in the pre-1945 period than they are now. In the post-war period there has been, as Raybould has ably shown, a marked and continuous differentiation in patterns of provision.

Raybould himself characterised the early British extra-mural work as follows:

a strong emphasis on liberal education, and an absence of concern with vocational studies or courses leading to examinations; within the field of liberal studies, the attaching of special importance to social studies; a particular care for the recruitment of 'educationally underprivileged' students; insistence on prolonged courses, directed private study, and a close tutorial relationship between teachers and taught; and on the organisational side, direction of the work by joint committees on which representatives of the WEA sat side by side with representatives of the universities.[12]

This is also the essence of Wiltshire's 'great tradition'. Both authors saw these emphases altering in the 1950s in response to changes occurring in society as a whole, and more particularly in higher education. Raybould saw the changes as follows:

the provision of an increasing number of courses with a strong vocational or semi-vocational purpose; the institution of extra-mural examinations and qualifications; the devotion of considerable resources to studies lacking any particular relevance to contemporary social affairs; the organising of many classes especially for undergraduate students and other students with a background of extended secondary, and often, higher education; a decline in the number of three-year courses, and a steady increase in the number of courses of less than one session's duration in which systematic private study is not a condition of membership; and organisational and administrative arrangements which put control of much of the work wholly or almost wholly into university hands, with little if any participation by representatives of students.[13]

Yet as reports of the extramural departments and of the Universities Council for Adult Education (UCAE) attest, it is still the 'liberal education of adults' and the liberal class-programme which remains the core of university adult education. This was the judgment of the Russell Committee:

> The essence of university extra-mural education is a weekly class meeting with a teacher able to bring the values of the university to the work and guide individual students in required reading, written work, and other exercises between meetings. As in all education, the quality of the work is variable.... The best classes, however, enable their students to think and work independently in the best traditions of university scholarship.[14]

Burmeister has been more explicit about some of the liberal values to which extramural work still aspires:

> The adult class is not merely an instrument of learning; it is a place where people from quite different backgrounds can together practise some of the virtues of democracy. In some way these small groups are replicas of society where the art of self-government can be practised. Ideally their members develop critical awareness, independence of judgement and skills of self-expression, all of which are so essential in a free society.[15]

On the face of things, therefore, it seems that the axial principles of university adult education are still to be found within the Great Tradition, despite the continued erosion of its basic precepts, and the steady diversification of university activities in this field. Yet criticisms of this tradition by now amount to such a familiar litany, and the attacks have been going on for such a long time, that in joining them one is likely to be accused of flogging a dead horse. It is now well known that the traditional tutorial classes account for a very small proportion of total enrolments, that these tend to appeal to an educationally privileged group, and that there is commonly a rather high rate of 'recidivism' amongst them. It is also firmly established that in an age when the 'reflective citizen' clearly needs to be well informed on science and technology in order to be able to understand many of the pressing political, economic and social problems of our time, the provision of ordinary extramural classes in the science-technology area is negligible. The hegemony of the liberal tradition has encouraged a narrow and restricted conception of adult education at a time when expansiveness of vision has been called for, and it has fostered an excessively individualistic approach to the task of educating adults.[16]

The Great Tradition has clearly lost its vitality and relevance, and is now a palimpsest, an echo, without a life of its own, and with no prospect of indicating the way ahead into the next century. Where then are new guiding principles to be found? Why is it so hard for them to become established? It is as though the foliage of some long established plant gets trampled and cut, and yet goes on trying to reproduce itself in the only way it can, like the tap root of some virile creeper. I have come to the view that the tap root of the liberal tradition has yet to be adequately identified and exposed, and it is for this reason in large part that liberalism continues to pervade the work, and that competing visions of the contribution that universities could make to the education of adults are stifled or squeezed to the periphery.

I believe furthermore that the axial principles of university adult education are the same as those of university education as a whole, and that it is the secondary, derivative characteristics of adult education work which give rise to the distinctions between the intramural and extramural teaching. Jepson says of the University Extension pioneers:

it was generally agreed among those interested in University Extension that the movement should aim to perpetuate the tradition of liberal education which for so long had been associated with the older universities. Emphasis was to be laid upon cultural rather than vocational education, upon humanistic rather than technical studies, upon developing the faculty of thought rather than the power to absorb factual information.[17]

Keddie, from a contemporary rather than an historical standpoint, argues that:

within a sociological frame of reference it becomes apparent that adult education is more like the rest of the education system than unlike it, both its curriculum and its pedagogy, and I shall treat the claim to distinctiveness as an ideological claim which requires explanation.[18]

This proposition runs counter to conventional wisdom amongst adult educators, that their work is of an essentially different kind from that of the internal teaching departments, and I will go to some lengths to demonstrate those basic respects in which it is in fact identical.

The central aspect of the liberal credo which has been neglected in the debate over its present worth and future viability is its epistemology, that is the theory of knowledge from which its structures and processes are, directly or indirectly, derived. Epistemology represents the 'genetic core' of educational enterprises, those deep seated basic assumptions which enter, usually unquestioned, into all the surface structures and daily routines of the enterprise; and it is here ultimately that we must look for new guiding principles if those we have inherited can no longer inspire confidence and commitment.[19]

Liberal adult education, along with university education as a whole, has long been committed to a single pre-eminent epistemology. What are its essential characteristics? How do these find expression in educational practice? Are there any worthwhile alternatives?

The Empiricist paradigm and its educational implications

The epistemology which has dominated western educational systems for the past three hundred years is Empiricist.[20] Only now that it is coming under severe attack from so many different directions can we begin to appreciate the full extent of its dominance, and its consequences for our ways of looking at, and thinking about the world. While it is in the state-controlled systems of secondary and tertiary education that this dominance is most complete and rigid, its influence has also pervaded primary and adult education, although greater diversity is evident in these arenas. Of our educational institutions it is the universities which are most heavily committed to this dying world view. University adult education consequently faces the difficult choice of clinging closer to the bosom of the conventional university and thereby drifting slowly into irrelevance, or David-like, challenging the Giant, prodding and provoking awareness of a new vision of reality, and new concepts of knowledge and learning.

While this Empiricist tradition has its internal conflicts and tensions, it also has some cardinal principles. The first of these is the Cartesian split of mind and matter, which posits an objective material world of things and events 'out there', accessible to observation and description, but always separated from and 'external' to the observer. A second, correlated assumption is that the things and events of the world operate mechanistically — that what we confront is a linear, continuous, Euclidean world of cause and effect, for which the analogue is the billiard table or the grandfather clock. This is the world of Newtonian classical mechanics. The third basic tenet is that of reductionism — the point of view that the way in which to understand complex or large-scale events and things is to analyse them into successively smaller units, until ideally we have a physico-mathematical explanation. It is this assumption which is responsible for the conventional hierarchy of disciplines as institutionalised in the Nobel prizes, and typically in university life. The cosmology of empiricism is the Great Machine in which, as Laplace argued, only a shortage of information stands between us and the ability to predict accurately every future state.

From an educational point of view the most important parts of the epistemology of Empiricism are its interpretation of perception and the acquisition of knowledge — its answers to the question, 'How can human beings come to know the working of the Great Machine?'

With regard to perception, the fundamental premise is that we do not, indeed cannot, perceive the world directly. The basic evidence for this view is the common fact that different people may form quite different impressions from a single episode or object, or that the same phenomenon may be experienced differently on different occasions by the same person. In short, perception is fallible, things are not always what they seem to be. So it is that conventional theories of perception all treat perception as a two-stage process: stimuli of one sort and another impinge upon our sensory receptors in the form of sense-data, these sense-data are then transmitted to the brain for processing into intelligible, meaningful information about reality. It has to be said that there is little agreement on the nature of the process by which sense-data are enriched or constructed into meanings. Broadly speaking, it is held that human beings get to know the world as a result of associations forming between the elements of sense-data that are collected. These are mentally constructed by processes of abstraction and generalisation, inference and deduction, into an ever more detailed and complex representation or 'mapping' of the actual objects and events in the world:

Abstraction is a crucial feature of this knowledge because in order to compare and to classify the immense variety of shapes, structures, and phenomena around us we cannot take all their features into account, but have to select a few significant ones. Thus we construct an intellectual map of reality in which things are reduced to their general outlines. Rational knowledge is thus a system of abstract concepts and symbols, characterised by the linear, sequential structure which is typical of our thinking and speaking.[21]

While the theory of learning which has stuck most faithfully to these empiricist precepts is of course associationism or behaviourism, the recently emergent cognitive and information-processing theories of learning share the same sensory concept of mind.[22]

The cosmology of mechanism and the theory of indirect perception are in turn closely associated with Empiricism's distinctive philosophy of knowledge — its answers to the questions 'What is knowledge, and how is it produced?' While Empiricism's core proposition is that all our knowledge is based upon or derived ultimately from experience, this is heavily qualified by the assertion that ordinary, every-day experience is a most fallible tool. Knowledge consists of true statements about the world, and has to be strenuously demarcated from myth, common sense, fantasy, fable, dreams and so forth. Given that our sense organs receive only attenuated representations of reality, great care is obviously required in constructing and following the rules by which the wheat of truth is to be separated from the chaff of accidental association, bias, idiosyncracy, and so on. Hence the norms of scientific enquiry, such as Merton's (Communism, Universalism, Disinterestedness, and Organised Scepticism), and the rules and conventions of the philosophy of science whereby propositions are to be supported and tested.[23] In practical terms the business of creating new knowledge demands detachment and objectivity, the ability to isolate and analyse by suitably controlled experiment or observation, and, in drawing conclusions, an appreciation of the logic of propositions. The progress of science is indicated by gradual extension of the area of stable, indubitable truths, as more and more of the scientifically unknown is explored and 'conquered'. This process is painstaking, arduous, slow and frustrating, and is the preserve of the highest intellects.

Adherence to this epistemology has some definite and predictable consequences for educational practice, of which the most decisive is that it issues in a subject-centred approach to teaching. Within the empiricist epistemology the educational enterprise as a whole is founded on the assumption that the classroom is the door to reality, that formal knowledge, accumulated, tested and integrated according to the canons of empirical science accounts for reality in so far as it is known, and therefore represents all that is worth knowing. The process of education therefore must start with the corpus of formal knowledge, and it is ultimately in learning and understanding what is in this corpus that the learner becomes an educated person.

The education process consists of four essential elements, and the relationships amongst them. There are choices in the way in which these relationships are established. In simple terms the elements that must be related are: the world, or reality — what there is to be known; knowledge — the record of descriptions, explanations, analyses of reality; teachers — those persons who have acquired knowledge of some aspect of the world and are in a position to pass this on to others; and learners — all those who are in the position of wanting, needing, or getting knowledge and understanding of the world. Empiricist epistemology, which informs the 'liberal education of adults', structures the relationships between these elements as shown in Figure 1.

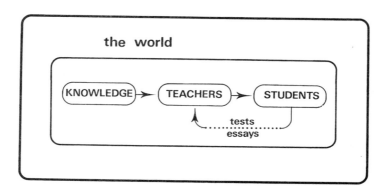

Fig.1

Because knowledge has had to be painstakingly collected and tested, and separated from the chaff of rumour, myth, common sense, dreaming, and so on, it is precious stuff, and not readily accessible to those who are ignorant of the special rules of enquiry and verification. A teacher — someone who has been formally trained and accredited in a subject — is therefore necessary to mediate between learners and the knowledge that they are to acquire; the learner has no direct access to knowledge of this sort. Because stable reliable truths about the world are by definition part of the subjects of geography, history, engineering, biology and so forth, then this knowledge is available in texts, and the process of education accordingly centres on the mastery of texts of one sort and another. The world is a source of distraction and interferences when education is defined this way, and we therefore go to great lengths to insulate the teaching environment from it by physical arrangements and by timetabling. When reality is introduced in to the teaching process it is in terms of examples or illustrations intended to vivify the texts and demonstrations, as in the case of excursions from school. The learner's progress is measured by ability to reproduce what the teacher imparts, by means of exams, written work, answering questions, and so on, and there is a perennial debate over the standards that ought to be set for such work.

Lawson's widely cited text on the philosophy of adult education puts it this way:

> Traditionally, the educator's authority and his right to exercise authority derives from his mastery of an area of public knowledge of which he is a representative. Without such an external frame of reference the concept of education as we know it is rendered meaningless because the whole enterprise is rooted in the belief in an objective knowledge beyond the opinion and prejudice of any single individual.... Once the authority of knowledge is questioned, it becomes difficult for the educator to retain his authority unless it is seen to be based on something other than knowledge.[24]

Within such a concept of education the relationship between learner and teacher is manifestly asymmetrical. Lawson is even more explicit on this point:

> the professional's opinions and value judgements must derive their validity from something other than the fact that they are his opinions and the key surely is that they are the opinions and judgements of a

professional. That is someone who subscribes to and is a representative of some value system, a code of behaviour, a set of standards and a body of knowledge and skills. In this respect the organiser and teacher derives his justification from whatever are regarded as educational values, educational knowledge and skills, and he is in a similar position to the lawyer, doctor and social worker.[25]

This concept of the relationship between the teachers and learners seems to me to put in its true light the rhetoric within the liberal tradition concerning student participation: 'It is therefore no accident, but an expression of an adult education philosophy which produces the student committee as a vital and indeed a primary feature of adult education institutions'.[26] The reality of this 'vital feature' is that the learner gets all the 'participation' in the educational process that the average patient gets from his or her doctor. What there is left to participate in when the authority and professionalism of the educator have been duly respected is the choice of tea or coffee and what time of day the class should start. To participate in the real business of the education process itself, apart from the peripheral logistic and social concerns, requires in this view that the learners be of special calibre:

> The assumption also has to be made that the members of a group are sufficiently articulate and possess an adequate vocabulary and conceptual framework to enable them to conduct a meaningful discussion. If these conditions are met then the validity of the student-centred approach can perhaps be recognised.[27]

Views such as this should by no means be treated as idiosyncratic expressions of opinion. They derive from a set of epistemological assumptions (of which the holders may lack awareness) which systematically structure educational systems and educational processes in the manner indicated in the model.[28]

The Contextualist paradigm and its educational implications

Empiricist epistemology has exerted a dominant though not an exclusive influence over educational practice. The signs are that the strands of an alternative, competing epistemology are at present being drawn together and articulated in a way that may well challenge this dominance. The necessity for such a shift is now very widely recognised and supported:

> We are trying to apply the concepts of an outdated world view — the mechanistic world view of Cartesian-Newtonian science — to a reality that can no longer be understood on these terms .... What we need then, is a fundamental change in our thoughts, perceptions and values. The beginnings of this change are already visible in all fields, and the shift from a mechanistic towards a holistic conception of reality is likely to dominate the entire decade.[29]

The major strands of this transformation are coming from ecological psychology, from developments in the philosophy of science and the sociology of knowledge, from experience in the human awareness movement and with eastern religion and philosophies. In terms of the challenge to empiricism however, the earliest and most decisive development has come in the 'new physics' of quantum mechanics, where in the heartland of the mechanistic world view, leading thinkers are coming to an entirely novel interpretation of the nature of our reality.

In his recent brilliant monograph, David Bohm, a leading theoretical physicist, argues that 'science itself is demanding a new, non-fragmentary world view', and using his understanding of relativity and quantum mechanics, goes on to propose one:

> The new form of insight can perhaps best be called Undivided Wholeness in Flowing Movement. This view implies that flow is, in some sense, prior to that of the 'things' that can be seen to form and dissolve in this flow .... The proposal for a new general form of insight is that all matter is of this nature: that is, there is a Universal flux that cannot be defined explicitly but which can be known only implicitly, as indicated by the explicitly definable shapes and forms, some stable and some unstable, that can be abstracted from the Universal flux. In this flow, mind and matter are not separate substances. Rather, they are different aspects of one whole and unbroken movement.[30]

The new cosmology that has been unveiled in quantum mechanics is a universe of unbroken dynamic unity, in which transformation — constant flow and change — is all-prevailing, and in which no sensible meaning can be given to the idea of an 'observer' detached from a world 'out there'. This universe is non-linear, acausal, discontinuous, and non-Euclidean.

At the same time as this new cosmology and its implications are being articulated and diffused, there is emerging a striking new theory of perception. As demonstrated by Emery, the breakthrough here has come with the development of an ecological approach to perception. This new theory of perception asserts that the environment for human behaviour has an information structure, and that human beings can extract information directly by means of perceptual systems which have evolved for this purpose, and which become 'tuned' to the environment by experience. The newborn is not a 'tabula rasa' at all, but arrives equipped with a set of overlapping perceptual systems which evolution has attuned for the obtaining of meaningful information directly from the environment. Unlike the 'sense organs' or 'receptor surfaces' of previous theories, these perceptual systems do not wait inertly for stimuli to impinge on them, but begin actively to mine the information present in the environment in a self-regulating quest for perceptual clarity. In this theory of direct perception the neuro-processing, construction stage of the causal theories of perception is unnecessary. Gibson, who has contributed much to this new approach, refers to it as the theory of 'information pick-up'.[31]

How within this new epistemology is knowledge to be created — what are the agreed procedures by which additions to the corpus of knowledge can be made? In some respects this very question becomes meaningless, because it refers back to the Cartesian partition between 'I' and 'the world', and the correlated notion that our ignorance of the Great Machine can be progressively conquered by scientific enquiry. The first point to emphasise therefore is that the old idea of objective knowledge of facts gathered with neither fear nor favour and available to all for corroboration, passes away. As Bohm puts it:

> One can no longer maintain the division between the observer and the observed (which is implicit in the atomistic view which regards each of these as separate aggregates of atoms). Rather both observer and observed are merging and interpenetrating aspects of one whole reality, which is indivisible and unanalysable.[32]

In place of the traditional idea of Absolute Truth come the more modest criteria of pragmatism, and thus an operational theory of truth: 'truth in terms of action, of actual events having references which lead to satisfactions in other actual events'.[33] The truth test of pragmatism is consistency with our experiences.

The inability to get apart from the world in order to study it 'object-ively' has decisive consequences for any existing principle of demarca-tion. Science becomes continuous with common sense, and with all other forms of knowing:

> Clarity of perception and thought evidently requires that we be generally aware of how our experience is shaped by the insight (clear or confused) provided by the theories that are implicit or explicit in our general ways of thinking. To this end it is useful to emphasise that experience and knowledge are one process rather than to think that our knowledge is *about* some sort of separate experience.[34]

In this alternative epistemology, which I am inclined to call 'context-ualist',[35] it is the world, reality, which has primacy in the educational process, rather than formal knowledge. More precisely perhaps, it is the 'learner-in-the-world', the experiences, challenges, problems, mysteries, and so on that motivate curiosity and inquiry. In this case it is curiosity itself that is precious, to be nurtured and protected, and the role of the 'teacher' (though one is more likely to find the vocabulary of resource person, leader, helper, facilitator, etc.) is that of nurturance. In practice this means moving alongside the learner, entering the learner's world, in order to be able to guide and support the further exploration of reality. The most important credential for this purpose is not a degree or a teacher's certificate, although these are not necessarily harmful, but the personal qualities that allow for the establishment of relationships based on mutual support and shared representation of reality, and a commitment to learning, rather than teaching. The facilitator in this process has an important role to play in inspiring and demonstrating the qualities of achievement and understanding to which learners might wish to aspire, but in the end the criteria for success or progress must be those of the learner. The necessary relationships are indicated in Figure 2 (overleaf).

Knowledge is not excluded from this model by any means, but it is better represented as a part, or dimension of reality, which is in principle open and accessible to all. It is of course an aspect of reality that a good facilitator will have awareness of and a lively interest in, but it is not a source of professional authority in the teaching-learning relationship. In this model too it is noteworthy that both the learner and the leader are part of the reality. This means that the learner himself or herself is an important and legitimate subject for enquiry, such that the quest for psychic, physical and spiritual integrity has a central place in the learning process. With the minor exception of the treatments given by counselling services to those who begin falling apart, our universities and colleges do not notably encourage learning of this sort. Within this contextualist epistemology there is an infinite number of valid ways of knowing the world. Valid representations of reality exist wherever people are able to satisfy their curiosity and make sense of their life situation, including where appropriate through the medium of formal disciplines.

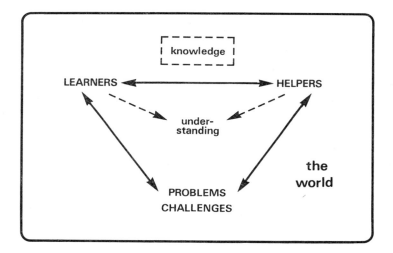

Fig.2

It is my contention therefore that the axial principles of university adult education are those of the universities themselves as they were found when the university extension, and later the extramural movements were initiated, and that adult education's distinctive features are in fact secondary, deriving from the social and political commitments of its founders, and certain beliefs about the learning needs and capabilities of adults. These secondary or derivative features are not therefore free-standing but are conditioned by the empiricist epistemology, and as a corollary cannot be successively modified or transformed unless there is a correlated change in the epistemological assumptions. I believe, as I have indicated, that important changes of the latter type are in fact occurring, and although they are at present confined to the margins and interstices of educational organisations they are likely to be intruding further into the mainstream of formal knowledge. To date there has been little sign of this type of debate within adult education as such, although all of the important issues have been most challengingly raised in the work of Paulo Freire.[36]

Rethinking adult education

If this analysis is at all correct, then we are likely eventually to see, and some may wish actively to promote, changes in the secondary character-istics of university adult education, and it is to these that I will now turn. With the misgivings of all who try to fit the real world into boxes, I will start by arranging these in a scheme, and then offer some explana-tion of the contrasts plotted in Figure 3.

ORIENTATION	Great Tradition	Emergent Principles
AXIAL PRINCIPLE	Empiricist	Contextualist
DERIVED CHARACTERISTICS		
institutional ideal	truth seeking	nurturance
basic role	service, provision	resource, catalyst
focus	individualistic, compensatory	communalistic, developmental
central tasks	teaching-organising	creating and managing learning settings

Fig. 3

73

The epistemology of empiricism embarks from the assumption of a split between mind and matter, thought and reality, and arrives at the view that knowledge is constituted of organised true statements about the world 'as it actually is'. More precisely, the *theories* which are the fruits of scientific investigation are held to give true knowledge of reality; the thoughts and the knowledge that thus become our represent-ation of reality are in a fundamental sense split off from and separate from this reality. The processes of observation and thought by means of which, in the different disciplines, reality may legitimately be codified into theories are the rules of scientific research.

The single most persistent and distinctive feature of the university as an institution is its efforts to monopolise and control these rules, and hence to demarcate between what is true and what is not true, or in the case of logical positivism, which statements are meaningful and which are meaningless. Teaching, the dissemination of these truths, has always been a secondary matter, and is not, as we know, distinctive of univ-ersities. Academic prestige and rewards relate most closely to discovery, and more importantly, to priority in discovery, as this is evidenced in formal publications. As a corollary, plagiarism, cheating, and the falsify-ing of data are the cardinal sins of academia. In order that the whole of reality should be rendered accessible and therefore susceptible to scientific enquiry universities have continuously propounded such values as the pursuit of knowledge for its own sake, the autonomy of universities themselves from external control, and academic freedom, protected by security of tenure.

In institutionalising the idea of knowledge as indubitable explanations of reality, discovered once and for all time, and the values of unfettered enquiry for its own sake, universities have been prone to arrogate to themselves *qua* institutions the right and responsibility to seek and defend the Truth. They somewhat lose sight of the fact that universities are a human product, designed by human individuals to meet human needs — to be in the service of human beings rather than in control of them. For understandable reasons, the pioneers and promoters of university adult education have been especially vulnerable to the myth that the university itself embodies the ideal of truth-seeking, and to the implication that the appropriate role for its members is one of faithful service to the institution.

Perhaps the clearest indication of this in the extramural tradition is the recurring, puritanical theme of learning as hard work — the imperative of 'thorough and systematic study', the idealising of those artisans who stumble to the class-room from the factory gates, the perennial soul-searching about 'standards' and the length of courses. This emphasis on learning as toil and sacrifice we may take as the hallmark of the theory of knowledge which tries so strenuously to differentiate knowledge from common sense and succeeds to the point that there is indeed often little resemblance. Behind these concerns lies a clear image of what it entails to be worthy of university education, and a fairly definite idea of the time and effort that ought to go into becoming a 'university person'. This nevertheless is presumed to be the most edifying aspiration for an extramural student.

Once the ideal of truth-seeking becomes institutionalised, embodying in a central way the university's idea of its own worth, the teaching mission becomes a matter of purveying these truths and cultivating the habits and attitudes of mind that account for their origins, and enable them to be put to use. In the early days, when these represented the dominant concerns of the universities as a whole, adult education emphasised 'liberal, humane studies', with some strong ideas about the particular virtues of a university education for the creation of disciplined, literate, and critical minds. This required exposure to and practice in the habits of logical, rational thought and argument — those paths to enlightenment that dwell at length on scholarly discussion and the writing of essays, and leave the learner well apprised of the civilising impact of Reason.

The assumption by universities that they monopolise the creation of truths and the virtues required to appreciate them enters into a second important characteristic of university adult education in Britain, which might be described as its service orientation — a perception of its essential role as a one-way provision, sometimes even as the imparting of a beneficence to the deserving poor. The essential point is that the teaching stance of the extramural, as of the internal, work has been didactic and pedagogic: it does not loom large in the philosophy or practice that the teachers might have much to learn from their students as far as their subject-matter is concerned, although the benefits to the soul are much referred to. This service orientation needs to be contrasted, as I will later on, with a resource, or catalyst orientation, which is based on differing assumptions about the capabilities of the laity to determine what they might want from their universities.

The service orientation obviously has its strengths, not least of which is the commitment to a continuing programme of sustained quality. On the other hand it is this service orientation that issues in the 'enrolment economy' and the endless dictates of The Programme, which can bog down even the most innovative spirits. It also is associated with a distinctive administrative and managerial style that tends to become routinised around an over-quantitative 'league table' mentality more geared to thrift than to enterprise, which finds it difficult to deal with learning possibilities that do not have a course as their outcome. This aspect of the liberal tradition is of course closely correlated with established funding mechanisms, and any substantial shift away from the conventional practice would require new thinking about revenue.

If the basic role has been one of service and provision, the focus of this service has been individualistic and compensatory.[37] In contrast with those who assert that education is, or at least ought to be, as neutral as a new coat of paint, I am in agreement with Freire's assertion that there is no such thing as a neutral education.[38] In the case of the 'liberal education of adults' it seems to me patent that its values and social purposes are those of a liberal capitalist society, and this is of course exactly what one should expect. Such societies stress and reward individual enterprise, and seek to create the conditions under which individual freedom to make informed choices is maximised — in the market place, at the ballot box, and in personal values and lifestyles. The good society is an aggregate outcome when such free and well-informed choices are the rule, and so the persistence of ignorance is a major stumbling block to its realisation. Ignorance therefore has to be conquered, for the good of ignorant individuals and for the good of society as a whole.

Liberal education is then about liberating from the bonds of ignorance :

Once education is defined in terms of the acquisition of public languages or public forms of knowledge which are regarded as the conceptual apparatus which makes rational thought possible, then those who are educated have been provided with the same means which will enable them to think, to analyse and to make judgements. They have acquired the attributes which make it appropriate to describe them as liberated or free men in the sense that the notion of 'liberal education' requires.[39]

The liberal philosophy stresses independence as a major outcome of the learning process — 'to think and work independently', 'independence of judgement' — and in its more extreme forms at least, is actively opposed to collectivist approaches, as in this argument from Paterson: 'I repudiate social change as an educational aim, for if adult education were to become harnessed to the promotion of a set of social causes, then it would become servile to those causes'.[40] This individualism may help to explain why university adult education does not play a larger part in addressing the complex issues and problems of societal management which seem, as Schön observes, to require so much 'public learning',[41] and why it is so nervous of becoming involved in community and organisational change projects. As Jackson notes: 'Even taking account of the theme of social commitment which runs through much British adult education history, the emphasis has been on developing the capacities of individuals rather than working with groups to solve collective problems'.[42] In fact the mainstream tradition has excluded such activities from its definition of education.

There is at least some consistency in the application of this individualistic ethic. Many of the university departments are themselves characterised by a management style of laissez-faire individualism which, especially when aided by distance, has fostered an extramural squirearchy with a way of life that is certainly 'fit for a gentleman'. In his solid enjoinder to 'go political or die', Thomas notes that political involvement and pressure group tactics are required: 'Such a course would be novel, and would ultimately mean some changes; for example the disappearance of the extra-mural tutor who models himself on the eighteenth century gentleman scholar'.[43] More importantly, for this pattern of behaviour is not at all typical, it is a management style which makes corporate planning — collective redirection and the setting of strategic objectives — virtually impossible.

The final dimension on which I wish to contrast the Great Tradition and the principles that are emerging within the contextualist epistemology is that of its central tasks. Jepson records that the Nottingham Memorialists insisted in 1872 that 'men who could attract and really teach working men must be thorough masters of their subjects and able not only to lecture, but also to discuss questions raised in class'. In order to defend the standards of its teachers the Oxford Delegacy determined in 1893 that:

If, after consideration, the application is provisionally approved by the Delegates, the applicant is required to submit in writing a syllabus of a course of not less than six lectures: the MSS., including title, should be of a length which would form, when printed, not more than fourteen pages of demy octavo. If the applicant's syllabus is approved, arrangements are made, as soon as practicable, for the delivery by him of one or more trial lectures.[44]

Things have changed a bit since then of course, not least in the fact that it would no longer be possible to apply such rigorous tests of the suitability of a lecturer! There has been a very welcome diversification of teaching methods and techniques, including the use of research projects, and various approaches to self-directed study. Nevertheless the norm is the presentation-discussion, or some variant of it, wherein the teacher as subject specialist presents or uncovers some aspect of the subject matter, and then enables the group to explore it further in discussion. This seems to me to be a normal, if not inevitable way to proceed 'once', as Lawson puts it, 'education is defined in terms of the acquisition of public languages or public forms of knowledge', or in other words the formal knowledge of the curriculum is taken as the starting point and the measure of educational progress. This, as we have seen, is not the only possible starting point. Even if one grants the particular priorities of liberal adult education, it seems to me that the concept of adult education as a sustained Socratic debate in small groups of common folk leans rather too heavily on the idea of the Great Teacher. This I presume is what Harold Wiltshire had in mind when he referred to the relative difficulty of the 'traditional work':

> we are likely to see more and more of our limited stock of money, time and talent given to the new work (which is relatively easy and socially acceptable) and less and less to the traditional work (which is relatively difficult and not obviously useful).[45]

To have Moultons and Hudson Shaws as one's heroes is not, unfortunately, enough to guarantee a department stocked with similar thoroughbreds. The reality is that in the discipline whose distinctive intellectual objective is to advance understanding of the learning behaviour of adults, the teachers show a normal distribution of talent for the task, ranging from the hopeless to the brilliant, and very few of them have either a special interest in or special understanding of the dynamics of adult learning. This raises some fundamental questions about who is to teach the teachers of an expanding adult education system, as well as raising some doubts about a concept of adult education which is so reliant on a supply of exceptional teachers.

These characteristics of the Great Tradition as it still permeates the field of university adult education — its Truth-seeking and subject-centredness, its service orientation and individualistic focus, its reliance on the presentation-discussion medium — are, I suggest, inter-related consequences of an adherence to the epistemology of empiricism. They are no more than a natural and logical outgrowth of this pre-eminent theory of knowledge. If, as I believe to be the case, a major overhaul of university adult education is required for it to survive and be useful into the next century, then it will not be enough to make piecemeal adjustments to the present guiding principles. The transformation needs to start at the level of the epistemology itself. I have sketched some of the contours of a newly emerging theory of knowledge, which I believe offers exciting new possibilities as a matrix for adult education, and will now consider the correlated changes in secondary principles that might be expected if contextualism were to come to the fore.

Obviously the epistemology of contextualism has nothing like the longevity and coherence of empiricism. The territory is somewhat new, inviting boldness, and a willingness to make mistakes. My approach to the task is to keep faith with the key elements of the alternative epistemology — its cosmology, its theory of perception, and its judgment on what is to be regarded as knowledge — and to seek to extract from these a new set of ideals and principles which might have survival value for university adult education over the coming decades.

Bohm's proposition of an implicate order of 'undivided wholeness in flowing movement' permits of no separation between mind and matter, consciousness and reality. These are divisions of thought which we have imposed on the 'holomovement', and are not to be confused, as is typically the case, with divisions in reality. In this view knowledge itself is part of the one total flux, it is not split off from and 'about' experience and reality, it is part of experience and reality:

only a view of knowledge as an integral part of the total flux of process may lead generally to a more harmonious and orderly approach to life as a whole, rather than to a static and fragmented view which does not treat knowledge as process, and which splits knowledge off from the rest of reality.[46]

The theories which summarise our understanding of the universe are forms of insight, a way of looking at the world, and not a form of knowledge of how the world is.[47] The pursuit of the truth, far from being the highest ideal, becomes a meaningless ideal, if it implies the formulation of indubitable propositions about reality as it actually is. Our quest should rather be to harmonise our insights with our lives, to seek their mutual improvement without splitting one from the other.

In revising his theory of ideal-seeking systems Emery abandons the ideal of Truth in favour of Nurturance, which implies that 'people will choose those purposes that contribute most to the cultivation and growth of their own competence and the competence of others to better pursue their ends'.[48] This ideal of nurturance seems to me entirely consistent with Bohm's prescriptions for how we might shift from fragmentation to wholeness. Emery goes on to say about the status of ideals in general:

I think that, in our present social turbulence, institutions like the universities, the courts and the churches deceive themselves if they insist that they are the true bearers of ideals. They may or may not be institutions that offer particularly favourable habitats for ideal-seeking individuals. However, so long as they insist on this deceit they denigrate the status of man. In practical terms they offer their rewards to those who are the most dedicated to serving the institution, not to the ideal seeking.[49]

If nurturance rather than truth is to become the guiding ideal for universities, it implies that knowledge should be sought not for its own sake, but for someone or something else, such that acts of enquiry are also acts of cultivation and growth. In this case cheating and plagiarism would become minor peccadillos; the greatest failure would be a lack of caring and support for others seeking to improve their insight and understanding. Consistent with this we could expect to hear a little less about the preciousness of university autonomy and academic freedom, and a little more about the accountability of both.

Within this scheme of things learning is no longer identified with toil and sacrifice, nor with the development of a single faculty. Instead one finds the re-emergence of ideas about learning which are more character-istic of preliterate societies:

> In an oral culture, verbalised learning takes place quite normally in an atmosphere of celebration or play. As events, words are more celebrations and less tools than in literate cultures. Only with the invention of writing and the isolation of the individual from the tribe will verbal learning and understanding itself become 'work' as distinct from play.[50]

Not only does learning become more like play than work, its focus spreads from the refinement of intellect to the development of the whole range of personal competencies and expressive faculties. As Emery puts it for example:

> If perception is so central to thinking and learning should we not be reconsidering the roles of art and poetry in education? Should we not be giving thought to the education that is to be gained from allowing that we might learn from the other senses, the haptic and those of smell and taste?[51]

Bohm makes the point in a slightly different way:

> My suggestion is that at each stage the proper order of operation of the mind requires an overall grasp of what is generally known, not only in formal, logical, mathematical terms, but also intuitively, in images, feelings, poetic usage of language, etc.[52]

Within the contextualist paradigm the basic role for adult education shifts from provision and service, to catalysing and resourcing. There is a tendency amongst the elders of the tribe to dismiss such notions as the trendy aberrations of the young and disaffected, who lack a sense of history. I think that they have to be taken much more seriously than this. The wall that has been erected over the past three hundred years between formal knowledge and common sense is now crumbling; respect-ed scholars and scientists from many backgrounds are legitimating the view that experience and knowledge are continuous, and not made of inherently different stuff. Gibson and his followers have shown that the assumptions of empiricism have seriously underestimated the 'wisdom of the body' with respect to the evolved potentialities of human percep-tual systems. These developments have some decisive implications for the educator:

> The new paradigm gives meaning to the phrase 'learning to learn'. In learning to learn we are learning to learn from our own perceptions; learning to accept our own perceptions as a direct form of knowledge and learning to suspect forms of knowledge that advance themselves by systematically discounting direct knowledge that people have in the life-sized range of things, events and processes. There is hardly a learning activity that is reconcilable with the concept of learning that is embedded in our current institutions of learning. They are committed to the view that learning is an indirect, esoteric and tortuous path of research with a split-off element concerned with transmitting the results to students. What is unavoidable in the study of nuclear particles and galaxies has become the prototype of learning.[53]

Within the alternative perspective it is absurd to conceive the main role of adult education in terms of the provision of courses distributed amongst the academic subject heads, and to measure success by number of enrolments. What is needed rather are ways of identifying the issues and challenges for individuals and groups that require further learning, and means for entering into collaborative relationships with them so as to stimulate and guide enquiry. Freire has called this role 'problematising' and the process that it initiates 'conscientisation'. A critical requirement of this approach is that the educator enters each new situation as a learner; unlike the 'banking' or 'nutritive' concepts of education there are no 'deposits' to be made.[54] At the institutional level, as for the individual teacher, there has to be openness to new relationships, a willingness to enter these with the humility of a learner, and a commitment to responding in terms that are meaningful to the other. A programme dominated by traditional classes cannot do this, if only because there are no staff available for such tasks.

Let me hasten to add that while I have joined the substantial criticism of the 'traditional work' I have not come across, nor would I support, any suggestion that it be abolished. The liberal class-programme has its value and its place, but this is no longer centre stage for most of the show. There is clearly some market for such work, though limited in size and social composition, and it should continue, with every effort to maintain diversity and improve the quality of the courses. I believe however that it should account for a smaller proportion of total resources, especially the time of professional adult educators, and that the resources thus released should go into other types of activity for which the universities are well equipped, and for which unmet demand already exists.

In this case the focus of activity would shift substantially to the communal level, as it is through communities, associations, organisations and other groupings that the problems and challenges of life are experienced, and within these groupings that the resources required for active adaptation are most likely to be found. Whereas a department devoted to the traditional class provision may appropriately go about its work by printing and publicising a programme of courses with the aim of attracting those individual men and women 'from all walks of life' who want to be taught a subject, a department which takes nurturance of learning as its ideal will be actively searching out and supporting those who are taking initiatives in learning and trying to identify those areas in which new learning is required if barriers to development are to be overcome. In practice this entails establishing and sustaining a network of directive correlations with community and occupational groups, trade unions, industry and commerce, government bodies, health and welfare systems, minority groups, and so forth, not as a means of gaining support and recognition for a programme of courses but as part of the *primary task* itself.

I am aware that in itself engagement of this sort is not a new departure; indeed community-involvement projects such as those at St. Anne's, Nottingham, in Liverpool and Southampton have broken a path which others have been pleased to follow. In his inaugural lecture Jennings makes the point that education for citizenship should be concerned with helping people to participate more effectively in decision-making processes:

One of the most effective ways of doing this is to work in cooperation with local groups — community associations, civic societies, neighbourhood action groups. The experience of the universities and the WEA in various cities, including Hull, suggests that there is a need for what might be called a consultancy service as well as for courses and seminars. To provide this we would need to bring together adult educators and colleagues from social science departments who were interested in such research fields as planning, housing and transport.

The enlightenment would be a two-way process as the people in the community are experts on the problems of living in their particular environments.[55]

What is new in my proposal is that it envisages a figure-ground reversal such that this kind of real-life adult learning becomes the primary task, the figural element, and the organisation of liberal classes becomes more of the sideshow that it ought to be. This prospectus for university adult education would be shared I believe by the authors of *Adult Education for a Change*.[56] It is perhaps necessary to stress that one is not advocating an exclusive diet of community and organisational development. While there may be work of this sort arising from the relationships established, there will in actuality be as many different approaches to learning as there are opportunities to think of them. The competent adult educator will have to become familiar with a wider portion of the spectrum of responses to learning needs.

The individualism of the liberal tradition has always had a compensatory dimension — a 'second chance' for those who missed education earlier in life, and a special concern for the educationally underprivileged of all types. In my view these commitments are today politically naive, especially in the leading role they continue to ascribe to the cultivation of intellect as a path towards social justice. I am with Wilby when he asserts:

> We must accept that education is an ineffective form of social engineering. We can then escape from the liberal blind alley by accepting two simple propositions. First, that if we want to redistribute wealth and power in our society, we should distribute it by direct political means. Second, we should see education, not as a means of redistributing the national cake, but as part of the cake itself.[57]

As far as the 'second chance' is concerned, this is in addition sociologically naive. There are very few left in our societies who have not had secondary education of some sort, and the commonest characteristic of those who leave at the first opportunity is a strong antipathy towards the whole structure of formal education. Lozanov has found it useful to coin the term 'didactogeny' to refer to the disease that many of these 'failures' experience — the dislike of learning that is induced by poor and inappropriate teaching methods.[58]

We come finally to the question of what would be the central tasks for the adult educator in a future of this sort. Any answer to this question must first recognise that all activities would be influenced by a basic underlying shift from commitment to teaching, to commitment to learning. This is only a trivial distinction to those who would believe that there is some rough comparability between what is taught and what is learned. Consider, however, the possibilities indicated in Figure 4. In

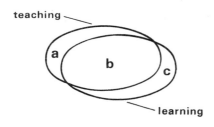

Fig. 4

fact, our educational institutions start with the assumption that: $b/a >> c/b$. Area 'a' is treated as an unfortunate waste of effort, and from time to time courses in teaching methods are given, or injunctions issued to try to reduce the size of this area. Area 'c' is ignored, as being of no interest to the teaching institutions. The long term goal for those with a primary commitment to teaching has been the progressive expansion in size of area 'b', by extending the years of schooling.

When learning becomes the prime concern, it is a matter of importance to eliminate teaching that does not contribute to learning, and which may harm it, and desirable to reduce the dependence of learning on the provision of specialised and necessarily expensive teaching. The long-term goal for those with a primary commitment to learning is the progressive expansion in size of area 'c' by enabling people to manage more of their own learning. The relationship sought is: $c >> b >> a$.

Within the conventional system the educator's task may be characterised as 'teaching-organising'. In the alternative system we would expect to see educators devoting most of their professional resources to working with others in the design and redesign of learning settings, to creating and managing the conditions under which others are most likely to be able to learn and to learn how to learn. If it is assumed that the knowledge which is worth having has in general already been collected together, codified and organised into texts, then it is perhaps sensible, and certainly expedient to standardise educational methodology around the core skills of teaching and organising teaching. On the other hand when reality, the issues and challenges of life become the starting point for learning, then our educational methodology has to be correspondingly rich and varied.

The concept of learning-settings does not therefore preclude formal lectures and presentations, nor does it refer exclusively to project work in structured, leaderless groups. It includes both of these and much more besides. The range of possibilities extends from the self-directed and contract learning approach so ably expounded and exemplified by Malcolm Knowles, to the design and management of very large scale conferences. It includes along the way the interesting recent developments in training and staff development practice of Megginson, Pedlar, Harrison, Channon, and others, the use of small groups for project work, and large scale action research. This of course is just to scratch the surface.[59] The point should perhaps be reiterated, that the adoption of such an approach to the tasks of adult education would require most of its practitioners to involve themselves in some pretty intensive staff development of their own, followed by a lifetime of on-the-job learning.

I am aware that examples can be found of each of the shifts that I have been discussing. The question that needs to be asked however, given the exhaustion of the Great Tradition, is why have they not diffused further and faster? My answer has been that such innovation and diffusion has been inhibited by a set of axial principles which were uncritically taken on from the universities in the beginning, which have biased the educational process towards transmissions of objective know-ledge of the universe as codified in academic disciplines. The role of empiricist epistemology as the genetic core of university adult education has been obscured by the stylistic emphases given originally to certain liberal and philanthropic values, and more recently by the preoccupation with the special characteristics of adults as learners. Neither of these emphases is anywhere near as fundamental to the character of university adult education today as its uncritical commitment to an empiricist epistemology, and only a transformation of these epistemological roots will generate the shift from education in truth-seeking towards the nurturance of learning that I have advocated. It remains to look at the implications of the contextualist paradigm for the structure and function-ing of university adult education in the future.

Extra-mural or anti-mural?

> The extra-mural departments fraternised with worthy adults who wanted to study the history of art, post-war economic development, or the sky at night, but because they were extra-mural departments they stood with their backs to the intra-mural departments — they faced towards the WEA and other extra-mural organisations.[60]

> the area at present loosely called 'continuing education' has a good claim to become the main point of growth within higher education in the eighties . . . . It follows that the adult or extra-mural or continuing education departments of the universities should, in the eighties, become much more central within their institutions.[61]

The concept and the stance of extramural work by the universities developed at a time when the uniqueness and the prestige of the universities was practically unchallenged. The work thus always had some of the qualities and the overtones of a Lord's philanthropy amongst the poor, and one sees in the universities the same mixture of motives which characteristically accompanies such benefaction. One concern, typifying those who actually do the work, is the genuine concern of the haves for the have nots, and a desire to do something about the situation. Another concern, typifying those who make the decisions, is that no more of the universities' resources should be allocated to such activity than is essential to maintain the good public relations that such investment can procure, and to satisfy the corporate conscience. This is simply an organisational fact of life, given that the essential business of the universities has long been defined as the education of undergraduate students and the conduct of research.

Today we find both the prestige and the uniqueness of the universities being thrown into serious question, at a time when, as I have indicated, a powerful new wave in adult education is about to break. This I believe is fertile ground for university adult education's fourth major structural development. It is time, as Hoggart argues, for university adult education to come in from the cold, and take up a position closer to the heartland of the university, from where the university as a whole can be engaged in giving substance to the move towards lifelong, or recurrent education.

It is the adult educators who must spark the debate on the future role of universities within a philosophy of lifelong learning, and take it into the highways and byways of university life. This I believe requires a new organisational base which straddles the boundary between the university and community, giving adult educators a firm footing in each and ease of movement between the two, without splitting the adult education enterprise.

The contrast between the familiar and what the future demands is best illustrated diagramatically. The traditional extramural organisation is shown in Figure 5.

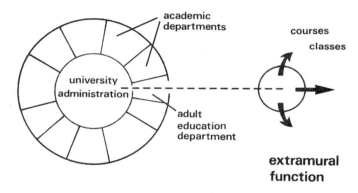

Fig. 5 'The moon model'

This we might call the 'moon model'. As far as the mother university is concerned it is a long way away, cannot be seen most of the time, and when it shines is only a reflection of the university itself anyway. Sometimes these moons have their own little satellites. These features may in times past have been strengths, at least potentially. If, as society seems to require, adult education is coming to mean the education of adults and universities are going to be asked to make their distinctive contribution to a 'learning society', then they are fatal weaknesses. Already one can see that more and more work in the continuing education field is being undertaken directly by the teaching departments that have the specialised resources required; it is not difficult to see how much more work could be done in this way. If it is left to the internal teaching departments, however, this new work is likely to be fragmented, opportunistic, and discipline based: the broader possibilities for re-education will be lost. In general, those departments with the strongest liberal tradition seem to be the most remote from possibilities such as these.

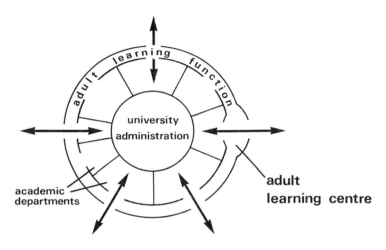

Fig. 6 'The membrane model'

The alternative, suggested in Figure 6, might be called the 'membrane model'. Here the adult education function has the character of a thin, translucent tissue which embraces and puts in touch with one another all the parts of the university; unlike a solid barrier it encourages flow and transfer from one side to another, and is itself transformed in such processes. Some centre — a critical mass — seems essential to this function, though its key role should be facilitative rather than executive. The critical transformation implied in these two models is from a situation in which adult education is the exclusive responsibility of a single specialised part that is for this purpose extruded from the university, to one in which it is a generalised function of the university as a whole, under the leadership and management of those with distinctive competence in such work. The pressure for such a transformation in practice comes and will come ultimately from the claims of new and different groups of adult learners from those who want to study the 'history of art or the sky at night', and growing pressure on the universities as such to broaden and diversify the benefits they return to their communities.

The opening-up of existing educational institutions is a corner-stone of any strategy for a system of continuing education. While the traditional extramural structure has been relatively effective in cultivating insights and techniques for the provision of adult education out in the community, it has been rather ineffective in mobilising the resources of the university as a whole for this community-service role, with the result that it tends to become cut off from the mainstream, marginal if not irrelevant to the fundamental questions of university government. The membrane model is designed for two-way traffic, of which the first element is increasing involvement of the internal departments in continuing education work of every sort — extension courses in relation to particular disciplines, public presentations of current research, conferences and workshops on issues of public interest, involvement of academics in community and organisational change projects, and so forth. This has basic implications for the role of the adult educator, to which I will return.

Greater openness is achieved both by getting more of the university out into the community, and by permitting more of the community entry to the university. The second element of the alternative model is expansion of access to the resources of the university as a result of continuing education activities, especially of access to study by mature age students without conventional academic qualifications. It has been observed that it is common for able 'graduates' of extramural classes to discover a brick wall when they want to start a degree course, or find themselves redirected to 'A' level courses.

The essential point to be made here is that those mature-age people who want and who can benefit from actual university-level education should get the real thing and not a substitute for it. There is no longer any question about the demand: CNAA degree enrolment went from 22,000 in 1972 to 132,000 in 1979; while up to 1978 the Open University had received a total of 329,639 valid applications (a proportion of which were repeat applications from unsuccessful applicants), but only a third of this number had been registered (of whom 35% had less than 'A' level qualifications). As guardians of the adult's right to learn, university adult education must push beyond such blandishments as the CVCP-TUC leaflet of 1978 and accept a major policy commitment to break down existing university attitudes to flexible mature-age entry and study conditions.[62]

Despite some welcome progress over the past few years, for which the spur has been enlightened self-interest, further action is urgently needed on such matters as:

(i) part-time undergraduate and graduate study as a normal option, and reorganisation of courses as necessary for this (Hull, Kent and Stirling seem to have shown the way here);

(ii) special mature-age entry schemes, including attention to science preparation courses, and automatic recognition of experience as an alternative to qualifications;

(iii) universal credit transfer within higher education;

(iv) optional accreditation throughout the system;

(v) paid educational leave and other measures of financial support for mature-age students, especially those married with children;

(vi) audit programmes, offering open public access to lecture courses where facilities permit;

(vii) advisory and counselling services for mature-age entrants.

If adult educators are to play a role in the expansion and diversification of opportunities for the public at large to share in the intellectual wealth of the universities then they will simply have to become better known, and better able to argue the case.

In making these points, I am aware of the organisational heterogeneity of university adult education, and am of the opinion that this in itself is a healthy state of affairs. The burden of my argument is that in order to make a virtue of membership of the university, university adult education should seek an organisational position from which it can 'invade' the university, and solicit maximum assistance in widening and deepening channels that run between it and the community. This amounts to a strategy for putting the university back into university adult education. It would be aided if the term 'extramural' were to be abandoned forthwith. It would certainly make an impression if some resources were redirected from tilling the land 'beyond the walls' to help take the walls down.

In organisational terms it seems to me that neither the conventional extramural structure nor the accoutrements of a normal academic department meet this requirement; the former is too insulated, while the latter sinks everything in becoming a member of the pack, and loses its claim to any co-ordinating or catalysing role. The ideal perhaps is a free-standing centre with a strong policy committee drawn from all parts of the university, with a charter for extending the whole of the operations of the university and an advocacy role in relation to the learning needs of adults, the communities, associations and organisations to which they belong.

Such a restructuring of the adult education enterprise is the first of two strategic innovations which I believe to be necessary to the future vitality of university adult education. The first is concerned with structure, the second with function, and the two are closely related. The traditional extramural organisational model is adapted to the provision of classes for consumption by individuals — this is after all the business that such organisations have specialised in. I do not believe that in the future university adult educators will be able to justify their livelihood on such a narrow functional base, and they should accordingly be looking seriously at the question 'what sort of business are we in?'

The consumption character of traditional class-programmes derives from the basic assumptions of voluntary, non-vocational, liberal adult education. The outcome of the process is individual enlightenment and personal development. As medical and dental services are consumed in the cultivation of healthy bodies, so adult education is consumed in the quest for healthy minds. Like medical and dental services, adult education is subsidised by the state. It is of course beyond question that certain programme areas in adult education will always have to be protected from market forces if they are to survive, and this will include some level of subsidy for the liberal class-programme. When the work of a department as a whole however is reliant on a single major source of grant, it may become susceptible to a 'subsidy mentality', with some of the following characteristics:

(i) loss of financial imagination — a sheer inability to perceive alternative funding possibilities, or inability to exploit them when they occur;

(ii) a management style more closely geared to careful administration and running a tight ship, than to speculation and innovation;

(iii) ignorance of the actual market value of the work that could be done, and of custom and practice in the continuing education market;

(iv) rigid over-conformity to administrative guidelines on how money can be spent; hiding behind the rule book.

I believe that not only will university adult education *need* to go out and earn if it is to upgrade and diversify its contribution, but also that there is a positive benefit in this. The first objection is always that he who paid the piper would call the tune. I believe conversely that there could be greater freedom of activity using earned income than currently exists in the spending of HMI-supervised grants, which force arbitrary judgements as to what is and what is not 'vocational'. In advocating a more entrepreneurial approach the sort of 'positive benefits' that I have in mind are as follows:

(i) it forces clients to think seriously about the sort of help or collaboration that they are looking for;

(ii) this enables adult educators to sharpen their perceptions of what is wanted and needed from them;

(iii) it is rewarding to staff to know that the world puts a tangible value on some of the work that they are doing;

(iv) the earned income creates a certain freedom to experiment and innovate.

There are dangers in over-dependence on the market-place, just as there are dangers in being overly reliant on subsidies or grants. The ideal might therefore be found in a 'mixed economy', in which up to a third of total income is derived from 'free enterprise' — enough to make a significant difference to the size and quality of total operations, but not so much as to make the acquisition of it an overriding preoccupation. As far as one can tell, the amount of earned income has been on the increase, and it is certainly likely to go on increasing. This trend will not only increase the degrees of freedom in planning future activities, but will stimulate the expansion of contracts with government and private organisations of every sort and lead to a fuller appreciation of the adult learning needs throughout our society.

Such a development might also encourage a shift in financial management from a consumption philosophy towards an investment philosophy, wherein more continuing education activities could be self-consciously designed to have a 'multiplier effect', to be reproductive of learning, in the same way that the best of the early extension lectures were. The subsidy mentality encourages a chivvying away at the carver of the cake; but once the cake is cut, the task is then to administer its distribution as fairly and as comprehensively as possible, down to the last crumb. The multiplier mentality encourages search for investment and 'spin offs', and the allocation of resources where they are most likely to be reproductive — to multiply. One aspect of this is a Robin Hood mentality, that is taking profits from those with high capacity to pay, in order to support work that cannot pay for itself otherwise. Other aspects might be:

(i) developing, and using learning techniques and methodologies which emphasise and support the growth of self-sustained independent enquiry, by groups and by individuals, such that an initial learning experience is more likely to promote others which do not depend on new resource allocation;

(ii) engaging with parts of the social structure in ways that increase the probability that those structures will permit, support, and encourage learning by those who participate in them (engendering social structures in communities and in organisations that are supportive of learning is a key element in making continuing education reproductive);

(iii) an approach to training in adult education which defines all on-going operations as learning opportunities and seeks to maximise the amount of 'learning by doing' that can be generated, by giving operational responsibilities to trainees whenever possible.

The role of staff: teachers or entrepeneurs?

If the six hundred or so staff of university adult education departments are to play a leading role in converting universities to some at least of the basic precepts of a system of continuing education, then substantial changes are implied for the traditional roles of such staff. Within the traditional extramural model a high proportion of them are subject-matter specialists whose responsibilities are formally accounted for by the DES convention that they should contribute something like 120 sessions of teaching each year. There are some major limitations of this staffing pattern:

(i) the existence of a subject-matter specialist within the adult education department can be used as an excuse, as well as an incentive, by the relevant internal department;

(ii) the multiplication of disciplines, and recent economic constraints, have made it harder and harder to cover the major academic areas, with the result that the disciplinary representation tends to become somewhat patchy and arbitrary;

(iii) the necessity to make teaching commitments months in advance, and the commitment to teaching in itself, leave little slack for responding to major public issues or chance opportunities as and when they occur;

(iv) it is a career cul-de-sac: with openings in the higher echelons of adult education as rare as they are elsewhere, and with little prospect of being able to return to discipline of origin, the subject-matter specialist in an adult education department has nowhere else to go.

In the light of the challenges ahead, and the size of the force available, I believe that the time of staff is too precious for so much of it to be spent on teaching. To put it simply, a far greater total of learning opportunities for adults could be generated by staff who spent more time on developmental work and less in classrooms. The ever-expanding total of graduates and professionally qualified people throughout our community, and the typically modest involvement of academics from other university departments, mean that there is ample scope for replacing full-time adult educators with part-time teachers, without any loss of academic respectability or reduction in the size of programmes. It should, I believe, become a policy commitment to have the universities define continuing education as a normal element of academic work, such that contribution to adult teaching is counted as part of the load, and no separate payment need be made for it. Even before this day arrives I believe a much higher level of participation from other departments could and should be generated, by adult education staff freed from some of their own teaching responsibilities.

However, this implies more than simply a reallocation of time — it implies a new style of adult educator with an 'entrepreneurial' approach to his task. An entrepreneur is a person with skills in assembling and integrating resources, including information, and applying these productively to the creation of new goods or services. We normally associate with this role such traits as a willingness to take risks, innovativeness, opportunism, and openness to change. If the challenge of mobilising the total resources of the university in the service of an expanding array of community needs and interests is to be met, then more of these 'catalysts' or 'animateurs' will be needed in adult education. The basic stock of knowledge is itself subject to constant change, and is unevenly distributed; the potential clients for learning diversify daily; the institutional fabric of post-school education seems to be in more or less constant flux. This scene requires some people who have a broad outline familiarity with existing knowledge, who have their ears to the ground as far as needs are concerned, and who know their way around the institutional system well enough to be able to mobilise resources as required. Though it is arguable that this should be a full-time job, there is some merit in the point of view that these staff should do enough teaching to retain a lively appreciation of the challenges of the classroom.

Instead of a long list of staff tutors, one could imagine a handful of staff in roles analogous to those of subject librarians in university libraries, with a general developmental responsibility for mobilising, for example, the science subjects — through lectures and seminars on topical research, post-experience and refresher courses, as well as liberal adult courses. Others would be freed to spend time meeting, consulting, and exploring future venues with community groups and organisations. The case for this sort of role has been previously stated by Caroline Ellwood:

> It is an advantage for both the university and society that there should be an identifiable body to act as a resource centre or matrix — not only to supply the demands of society, but itself to actively create a community of intellectual collaboration. Somewhere in the university

(polytechnic) there should be a body of people whose job it is to develop a dialogue between groups; to form a creative centre of real human responsibility; to bring together organisations; to bridge conceptually and assay current trends; to produce informed awareness of technological progress. Such a function is but an extension outwards of what the university as a whole is about.[63]

I am not arguing that *all* posts should fit such a job description. I am arguing that all departments should incorporate skills of this sort, and that the value of such entrepreneurial work should be recognised as intrinsic to the practice of continuing education within universities. One of the healthy side-effects of moves in this direction might be a greater respect by academics in adult education for the work currently done by administrative staff, and a progressive breaking down of the status and income barriers between these two groups which are still so common. This in turn will throw into sharp relief the prevailing sexual division of labour, and we may eventually see more female academics and more male receptionists and typists.

Towards a comprehensive university?

It cannot be denied of course that the pervasiveness of empiricist epistemology throughout university education is a serious constraint on the capacity of adult education departments to adopt an alternative theory of knowledge, and hence to diverge from the traditional assumptions of university teaching. It seems to me however that the critique of these assumptions is gathering force, and that adult educators should join and support it. As Kuhn observed, it is more likely to be the younger, more marginal staff with unconventional backgrounds who will be most able and willing to press the claims of the competing epistemology, and those who have been most fully socialised into traditional academic standards and values who will dig in and defend the faith.[64] If history is any guide the debate between champions of these competing paradigms is likely to be a picture of earnest people talking past one another, and in my view those who desire to see the new paradigm competing effectively will better spend their time *doing* it than arguing for it.

In seeking to transform the university itself, adult educators do have some useful points of leverage. That these have not so far been more fully exploited is due to the fact that there has been no strategic objective to aim for — the future scenario of university adult education has been 'business as usual', albeit with an increasingly defensive stance.

It is now widely acknowledged that the Russell Report, which could, and arguably should have done something about this, did not. Limited by terms of reference to 'non-vocational adult education' and (apparently by its own decision) to the next five years, it was an opportunity lost as far as long-range planning was concerned. The submission to it by the universities *via* the Universities Council for Adult Education boils down to a series of more or less enlightened administrative recommendations, and singularly failed to crystallise any new sense of purpose.[65] But for the subsequent DES discussion paper on higher education and the lure of its cherished 'Model E', I suspect that 1919 would still be a more significant date for adult education than 1990.[66]

The first and most obvious opportunity for adult education to engage the university about its broader purposes arises from the challenging new strategies that emerged out of the 'world education crisis' of the 1960s — lifelong, permanent, or recurrent education. Although the implications of these more comprehensive educational concepts for adult education were being pointed out a decade ago,[67] the OECD review of educational development strategy in England and Wales found it necessary to criticise both the 1972 White Paper and the Russell Report for their almost complete neglect of the concept of recurrent education, and there is little evidence yet of attempts to conceptualise, let alone implement a new role for universities in such a system.[68]

Schuller has clearly articulated the kind of developments that would be needed in the higher education sector.[69] In addition to the most basic requirement for widened and easier access, action is needed positively to stimulate new demand (following the example of the Open University and the Literacy Campaign), to attack credentialism, to introduce more non-degree work in higher education, and more diagnostic, introductory and bridging courses, and to introduce problem-centred approaches to learning. As Schuller points out, most of the elements that would be necessary in creating a system of continuing education for Britain are already present, a range of them already running into serious under-utilisation for demographic reasons. What would be required therefore is not a vast new expenditure on educational infrastructure, but some rather fundamental innovations in such areas as access, paid educational leave and other forms of study support, agency collaboration, advisory and counselling services, and so forth — a thorough reconceptualisation of the purposes of the existing educational system and of the criteria for using it.

In the second place it is arguable that the disinterested interplanetary visitor, observing our educational system in the initial convulsions of adapting itself to a strategy of lifelong learning, might conclude that there was a role for the universities in contributing to the continued learning of those whom they graduate, whose knowledge now so quickly becomes incomplete or obsolete. What this might mean in practice is that alongside the Master's, Doctor's and other accredited forms of postgraduate education there would be a positive flourishing of extension activities geared to the needs of particular professional or other occupational groups, or particular types of organisations (local government, the electronics industry, leisure clubs and so on). The generic character of such learning activity is its focus on the nexus between disciplines and occupations or between theory and practice, and the intent to improve practice through its confrontation with knowledge. While this comes naturally to a good adult educator, it is a foreign, and sometimes distasteful approach for the academic subject specialist within the empiricist paradigm of knowledge. There is accordingly a necessary role for the adult educator in translating between disciplines and practices, and in designing learning-settings that will provide for interaction and exchange of meanings and experiences, as well as pronouncements.

Finally, I believe that the time may be ripe for pressing the universities to become more conscious of their local and regional role, and that there is a very significant part for adult educators to play in this direction. The case has of course been stated before. In 1973 James concluded from his reflections on the establishment of a new university adult education centre at Surrey that universities have more to contribute to their regions than most of them are aware of, and that the involvement of the whole university is both possible and desirable.[70] This is presumably the premise on which Sussex and Lancaster too adopted structures for mobilising the whole university to be involved in adult and continuing education. Hoggart argues that through their adult education activities 'and through the fuller assumption of their role as the foremost intellectual centres within their areas, the universities could enter an era in which their sense of belonging to their local communities was better fulfilled'.[71]

In his bold and challenging advocacy of the 'comprehensive university' Pedley takes the argument much further.[72] His concept of a series of multi-institutional, open-access, regional campuses in fact takes towards their logical conclusion the implications of the contextualist paradigm for post-school education, and in my view has the value of a bench-mark against which our progress towards the nurturance of learning might usefully be measured in institutional terms.

In the final analysis, the argument for such a development is a pragmatic one. Respect and support for the universities is declining, while the communities in which they are established face increasing turbulence and instability. If universities could individually prove their worth in their own parishes, then collectively they may again find favour at the Exchequer.

Conclusion

Today, three different elements of adult education work can be found within the university sector. The largest and dominant of these has been the 'extramural studies' element, the provision of university-level, liberal, non-vocational courses for adults in the university's region. Nearly 60% of the 600 or so staff in university adult education are supported by the DES (at the rate of 75% of salary) in order to do this type of work. Secondly, some universities have a 'Department of Adult Education', signifying a commitment, *via* research and teaching, to the development of adult or continuing education as a field of intellectual enquiry. The 230 or so staff who are UGC-funded are presumably expected to be making a contribution in this area. The smallest and newest element is called continuing education, or extension studies, which connotes the role of catalyst vis à vis the university as a whole, and a commitment to deploying the university's resources throughout the community. Only a handful of universities are doing anything very substantial in this third area.

My argument is simply that these present priorities should be reversed, and that the continuing education, or extension element should become the essential distinguishing feature of university adult education. If the traditionalists wish to maintain the dominance of the liberal class, extramural element, then they will have to show why such a limited resource for adult education should be allocated to subsidising recreational learning of a small and educationally privileged group. The facts of the matter are in stark contrast to much of the rhetoric about 'second chance' and 'working class' education. I believe that provision of this sort is appropriate and worthwhile, and should be part of a university's contribution to the cultural life of its region. I am not at all convinced, however, by the propoganda one reads concerning the mysterious and profound processes of self-discovery and enlightenment that are supposed to take place in adult courses of this sort, and do not therefore see this type of provision as much more than a fiscal and administrative operation. Of itself, this type of provision does not require, or justify, a separate academic department.

If on the other hand, the major role of universities in adult education lay in the area of research and teaching, it would be absurd for such a scarce resource to be spread so thinly across the campuses. The UGC appointments would be better concentrated into half a dozen Faculties or Institutes of Continuing Education, in which a concerted thrust could be given to research and development leaving the DES-supported staff to work with the WEA and other agencies in the provision of liberal classes.

On the basis of this analysis, the only sound reason for maintaining groups of professional adult educators in each university has to be derived from the *extension* task, the task of mobilising resources throughout the university for community service of one sort or another. A reallocation of priorities and resources which made this the starting point and foundation of the universities' work in adult education would I believe be consistent with the move towards a national strategy and philosophy of continuing education as asserted by ACACE, and with the needs and interests of adult learners in contemporary society.

Notes and references

1. Thomas Kelly *A History of Adult Education in Great Britain* (Liverpool University Press, 1970), p. 216.

2. For the concept of 'appreciation' see Geoffrey Vickers *The Art of Judgement* (Chapman and Hall, 1965).

3. The concept of a 'lookout institution' is discussed in J. Jantsch *Perspectives of Planning* (Paris: OECD, 1969).

4. Advisory Council for Adult and Continuing Education (ACACE) *Continuing Education: from policies to practice* (Leicester: ACACE, 1982).

5. ACACE *Towards Continuing Education* (Leicester: ACACE, 1979).

6. For two recent surveys of the entire gamut of British adult education see Bernard Jennings *Adult Education in Europe: United Kingdom* (Prague: European Centre for Leisure and Education, 1981) and Derek Legge *The Education of Adults in Britain* (Milton Keynes: Open University Press, 1982). For a reasonably up-to-date and comprehensive survey of post-school education provision see M. Locke and J. Pratt *A Guide to Learning after School* (Penguin Books, 1979), Tyrell Burgess *Education after School* (Penguin Books, 1977) and Russ Russell *Further Education in England and Wales* (Coombe Lodge Working Papers, November 1979).

7. Bernard Jennings *New Lamps for Old? University adult education in retrospect and prospect* (Inaugural lecture, University of Hull, 1976).

8. I have adopted the idea of 'axial principles' from Daniel Bell *The Coming of Post-Industrial Society* (New York: Basic Books, 1973). A fuller spelling-out of the organisation theory underpinning this analysis can be found in J. E. T. Eldrige and A. D. Crombie *A Sociology of Organisations* (Allen and Unwin, 1974), P. G. Herbst *Alternatives to Hierarchies* (Leiden: Nijhoff, 1976) and Philip Selznick *Leadership in Administration* (New York: Harper and Row, 1957).

9. *Concise Oxford Dictionary* (4th edition, 1951).

10. M. Stephens and G. Roderick 'Adult education and the community university' *Adult Education* 45 (1972), pp. 138–42.

11. H. Wiltshire 'The Great Tradition in university adult education' *Adult Education* 29, (1956); A. R. Rogers (ed.) *The Spirit and the Form* (University of Nottingham, Department of Adult Education, 1976).

12. S. G. Raybould *University Extramural Education in England 1954–62* (Michael Joseph, 1964), p. 13.

13. Raybould (1964), p. 13.

14. Advisory Committee on Adult Education *Adult Education: a plan for development* (HMSO, 1973) (The 'Russell Report'), p. 36.

15. W. Burmeister quoted in J. Burrows *University Adult Education in London: a century of achievement* (University of London, 1976), p. vii.

16. For critical appraisals of liberalism in adult education see Caroline Ellwood *Adult Learning Today: a new role for the universities?* (Sage Publications, 1976) and J. L. Thompson (ed.) *Adult Education for a Change* (Hutchinson, 1980).

17. N. A. Jepson *The Beginnings of English University Adult Education* (Michael Joseph, 1973), pp. 215–6.

18. Nell Keddie 'Adult education: an ideology of individualism' in J. L. Thompson (1980), Ch. 2.

19. For the concept of 'genetic core' see the superb analysis of the logic of bureaucracy in Herbst (1976), and for its relevance to educational systems the same author's *Socio-Technical Design: strategies in multi-disciplinary research* (Tavistock Publications, 1974).

20. Essential background to this epistemological analysis is to be found in F. E. Emery 'Educational paradigms' *Human Futures* (Spring 1981), pp. 3–19.

21. F. Capra *The Tao of Physics* (Boulder, Colorado: Shanbhala, 1975), p. 27.

22. W. B. Weimer 'A conceptual framework for cognitive psychology. Motor theories of the mind' in R. Shaw and J. Bransford (eds) *Perceiving, Acting and Knowing: toward an ecological psychology* (New Jersey: Lawrence Erlbaum Assocs, 1977), Ch. 10.

23. R. K. Merton *Social Theory and Social Structure* (New York: Free Press, 1957).

24. K. H. Lawson *Philosophical Concepts and Values in Adult Education* Revd ed. (Milton Keynes: Open University Press, 1979), pp. 89–90.

25. Lawson (1979), p. 21.

26. Lawson (1979), p. 20.

27. Lawson (1979), p. 24. On the differences between such psuedo-participation and genuine participation in learning see A. D. Crombie *Participation and Recurrent Education* (Nottingham: Association for Recurrent Education, 1980).

28. For a fuller exposition of these relationships in education systems see Crombie (1980).

29. F. Capra 'The turning point. A new vision of reality' *The Futurist* 16 (1982), pp. 19–24.

30. David Bohm *Wholeness and the Implicate Order* (Routledge and Kegan Paul, 1980), p. 11.

31. Emery (1981) attributes the key breakthrough to F. Heider *The Psychology of Interpersonal Relations* (New York: Wiley, 1958) and *On Perception and the Event Structure and the Psychological Environment: selected papers* (New York: International Universities Press, 1959), James Gibson *The Senses considered as Perceptual Systems* (Boston: Houghton Mifflin, 1966) and *The Ecological Approach to Visual Perception* (Boston: Houghton Mifflin, 1979). For an excellent consolidating work on the theory of direct perception see C. F. Michaels and C. Carello *Direct Perception* (New Jersey: Prentice Hall, 1981).

32. Bohm (1980), p. 9.

33. S. C. Pepper *World Hypotheses* (University of California Press, 1942), p. 268.

34. Bohm (1980), p. 6.

35. I have borrowed this term from S. C. Pepper (1942): Contextualism is one of his four 'world hypotheses'. A re-reading of Pepper's Ch. 10 confirms the appropriateness of this term for present purposes.

36. Paulo Freire *Pedagogy of the Oppressed* (Penguin Books, 1972), *Cultural Action for Freedom* (Penguin Books, 1972) and *Education: the practice of freedom* (Writers and Readers Publishing Co-operative, 1973).

37. For a more detailed analysis of this aspect see Keddie in Thompson (1980).

38. Freire *Cultural Action for Freedom*.

39. Lawson (1979), p. 103.

40. R. W. K. Paterson 'Social change as an educational aim' *Adult Education* 45 (1973), p. 358.

41. Donald Schön *Beyond the Stable State* (Temple Smith, 1971), Ch. 5.

42. Keith Jackson 'Adult education and community development' *Studies in Adult Education* 2 (1970), pp. 156–79.

43. J. E. Thomas 'Go political or die' in K. Lawson (ed.) *Crisis in Education* (Nottingham: Save Adult Education Group, 1979), p. 19.

44. Quoted in Jepson (1973), p. 246.

45. Wiltshire (1956), p. 96.

46. Bohm (1980), p. 63.

47. This point of view is well developed by Herbst (1974) as the 'multiple perspective' map of knowledge.

48. F. E. Emery *Futures We Are In* (Leiden: Nijhoff, 1977), pp. 74–5. See also the same author's *In Pursuit of Ideals* (Canberra: Centre for Continuing Education, 1976).

49. Emery (1977), p. 80.

50. Walter J. Ong *The Presence of the Word* (New York: Simon and Schuster, 1967), p. 30.

51. Emery (1981), p. 14.

52. Bohm (1980), p. xiv.

53. Emery (1981), p. 14.

54. Freire *Pedagogy of the Oppressed*, Ch. 2.

55. Jennings (1976), p. 19. See also P. Fordham *et al. Learning Networks in Adult Education* (Routledge and Kegan Paul, 1979) and Tom Lovett *Adult Education, Community Development and the Working Class* (Ward Lock Educational, 1975).

56. Thompson (1980).

57. Wilby quoted in Thompson (1980), p. 10.

58. S. Ostrander and L. Schroder *Superlearning* (Sphere Books, 1981), p. 32.

59. See Malcolm Knowles *Self-Directed Learning* (Chicago: Follett Publishing Co., 1975); D. Megginson and M. Pedler 'Developing structures and technology for the learning community' *Journal of European Training* 5, (1976), pp. 262–75; R. Harrison 'How to design and conduct self-directed learning experiences' *Group and Organisational Studies* 3 (1978), pp. 149–67; J. B. Channon 'Work settings' *Military Review* 56 (1976), pp. 74–87.

60. W. A. C. Stewart 'The university's commitment to adult education' *Adult Education* 43 (1970), p. 110.

61. Richard Hoggart *After Expansion: a Time for Diversity. The universities into the 1990s* (Leicester: ACACE, 1978), pp. 5, 9.

62. *Mature Students. A brief guide to university entrance,* published jointly by the Committee of Vice-Chancellors and Principals and the Trades Union Congress, Spring 1978.

63. Ellwood (1976), p. 229.

64. T. S. Kuhn *The Structure of Scientific Revolutions* (University of Chicago Press, 1962).

65. Universities Council for Adult Education *University Adult Education in the later Twentieth Century* (Birmingham: UCAE, 1970).

66. Department of Education and Science and the Scottish Education Department *Higher Education into the 1990s* (HMSO, 1978).

67. E. K. T. Coles 'Universities and adult education' *International Review of Education* 18 (1972), pp. 172–82.

68. M. Niveau *et al. Educational Development Strategy in England and Wales* (OECD Reviews of National Policies for Education, 1975).

69. T. Schuller *Education through Life* (Young Fabian Pamphlet 47, 1978).

70. D. James 'Birth of a university adult education centre' *Studies in Adult Education* 5 (1973), pp. 124–42.

71. Hoggart (1978), p. 9.

72. R. Pedley *Towards the Comprehensive University* (Macmillan, 1977).